Making Dances That Matter

Making Dances

That Matter

RESOURCES

FOR COMMUNITY

CREATIVITY

ANNA HALPRIN

with

RACHEL KAPLAN

WESLEYAN UNIVERSITY PRESS

Middletown, Connecticut

Wesleyan University Press

Middletown CT 06459

www.wesleyan.edu/wespress

Manufactured in the United States of America

Typeset in Miller and Didot by Tseng Informations Systems, Inc.

Title page image © Jay Graham Photographer. Anna Halprin Papers;
courtesy of Museum of Performance and Design, San Francisco

Library of Congress Cataloging-in-Publication Data

Names: Halprin, Anna, author. | Kaplan, Rachel, 1963– author.

Title: Making dances that matter: resources for community creativity /
    Anna Halprin with Rachel Kaplan.

Description: Middletown, Connecticut: Wesleyan University Press, [2018] |
    Includes bibliographical references and index.

Identifiers: LCCN 2018023905 (print) | LCCN 2018030717 (ebook) |
    ISBN 9780819575661 (ebook) | ISBN 9780819578440 (cloth: alk. paper) |
    ISBN 9780819575654 (paperback: alk. paper)

Subjects: LCSH: Halprin, Anna—Criticism and interpretation. | Dance—
    Social aspects. | Postmodern dance—United States.

Classification: LCC GV1785.H267 (ebook) | LCC GV1785.H267 H35 2018 (print) |
    DDC 792.8092 [B] —dc23

LC record available at https://lccn.loc.gov/2018023905

5 4 3 2 1

For my daughters,

DARIA *and* RANA HALPRIN,

for their continued support and participation

CONTENTS

INTRODUCTION

When I was a little girl, I would go with my parents and my older brothers to visit my grandparents, who lived on the west side of Chicago. When we arrived, I would run as fast as I could down the street to the synagogue to see my grandfather. I sat upstairs in the balcony, where all the women sat. As I looked down at my grandfather, I saw all the men in long black coats, yarmulkes, and white-and-black-striped shawls over their heads. I never saw anything like this in the middle-class, predominantly Anglo-Saxon suburb of Winnetka, Illinois, where I grew up. Everything about the synagogue was awesome and wonderful to me. As my grandfather prayed, he chanted in Hebrew and swayed back and forth. As his prayers intensified, he would clap his hands, fling them into the air, and jump about. Although I didn't understand what he was saying, I felt his voice and his movements within my body. I felt his passion and his heart, and I understood intuitively that he was dancing.

His dance expressed intense emotions—sadness, anger, exhortation, joy, and ecstasy. I had never seen anyone dance that way before. It was free and wild and uninhibited; it was fun and spontaneous and emotional. I didn't feel like this when I went to my dance classes, or to Sunday school! After he finished, my grandfather and I would meet at the door. He would be glad to see me and lift me into the air and hug me. Then he would hold my hand and we would walk slowly back to his house. I could tell by the way he touched me that he loved me. I was so happy I would skip and gallop down the street with him at my side. I believed that my grandfather, with his white silky hair and his long white beard, was God and that God was a dancer.

The memories of my grandfather's love, his dance, and his ritual have been with me all my life. I believe that what I have been doing as an adult is trying to recover the means by which I could experience a dance of such spiritual power and meaning. I didn't inherit the same customs, community, or clear social roles my grandfather did. I can never live like him or do his dance with that sense of authenticity and devotion, but I have been driven to find a dance that moves me and the communities I work with as much as his dance moved him.

We may no longer have the kind of clear, if unspoken, agreements about the meaning and function of dance that my grandfather and his community did, but I believe we are still drawn to dance as an expression of our humanity. The diversity of dance forms we do have—folk, ethnic, ballet, modern, postmodern, jazz, tap, and street dances of all sorts—is a testament to the enduring human need to express ourselves through movement. As a longtime dance artist, my interest lies in reinvigorating our relationship to dance so that it once again serves our lives in substantive and essential ways. Throughout history, people have danced their most profound needs and struggles as a means of reaffirming harmony with themselves, with each other, and with the natural world. For traditional peoples, dance and all the arts provided an important language, communicating ideas about power, spiritual matters, and the natural world. Before written language, dance was an essential part of the oral tradition, a way of passing morals, ethics, and story from generation to generation. For thousands of years, dance has played an important role in forging collective identities among cultural and ethnic groups throughout the world. Through dance, people have marked major life transitions, from birth through initiation into adulthood to death. Dance has allowed people to vent strong emotions, such as grief or anger, as well as to express love and gratitude; and it has helped motivate community members to cooperate. Dance contributes to social cohesiveness and provides a venue where people can enact spiritual rituals and beliefs. Part of the challenge I have faced in my work is to take our practice of mostly ornamental or performative dance to a place where it can serve multiple community, social, and survival needs. This is a book about creating dances that matter to people in their real lives, repurposing dance as a vehicle for social change and community resilience.

Although dance has to a great extent been emptied of its range of meaning in our modern world, I have been lucky enough to witness how it can still bring communities together to encounter issues that may be overwhelming, unresolved, destructive, or even life-threatening. Over many decades, I have danced with a variety of people—seniors and youngsters, people of different ethnicities and racial backgrounds, the able-bodied and the disabled, trained dancers and everyday movers—using dance as a vehicle to explore our stories, create community, heal our wounds, mourn our losses, and celebrate our victories. I have been searching for dances that can define our values, unite us, and help us express our full emotional range. Through a collaborative process called the RSVP Cycles, which my husband, Lawrence Halprin, and I evolved over many decades of practice, I have tried to create dances that facilitate our search for both an individual and collective identity in the present moment. In essence, that is what this book is about—learning how to create dances that are responsive to the present moment while binding together and healing our communities.

One of my central intentions is to create dances that change the dancer and, in so doing, affect our personal, social, and cultural lives. In this urgent time, it is more important than ever that we use all the resources we have—whether they are artistic, political, service-oriented, or educational—to heal our families, our communities, our land, and ourselves. Dance and art offer primary ways for people to access their inner and collective power. We can use art expressions to contain, express, release, and heal our fears and motivate us toward social change. Movement expresses universal human responses through a vehicle we all share—the expressive, mysterious, complex human body. Dance puts us into relationship with one another and our environment, reaching into the depths of our beings and reflecting this knowledge back to us. Dance is an immediate, direct, and powerful force that bypasses discussion, argument, and difference. We all breathe; our hearts beat; we need air and water to live; we love; we fear; we suffer—all through the vehicle of our sacred bodies. Through dance, we can use our individual resources and our collective experiences and narratives to subvert the isolation of our culture and build a collective response truly answerable to our human needs.

My work and my perspective have been influenced by the dances of indigenous peoples. One event that intrigued and deeply moved me was a Corn Dance I witnessed in the Santo Domingo Pueblo, near Santa Fe, New Mexico. The Corn Dance can go on for five days and nights before being completed. The dancers perform their repetitive steps over and over for hours and hours, day after day, until they finish their tasks. Often described as a rain dance, a rite of renewal and purification, its full meaning is known only to the Pueblo participants. What I witnessed was something deeply *committed* in this dance, the moving fierceness of the dancers' intent. I am interested in creating participatory dances as captivating as this ceremony, and as essential. The expansion of time in such ceremonies, the commitment to the ritualized activity *no matter how long it takes*, moves these events out of the realm of the mundane and places them in the realm of the sacred.

My grandfather was fortunate in that he had a ritual that connected him to his people and his community, and in turn sustained his Jewish culture. Many of us do not have this kind of dance ritual or active tradition in our lives. We live in a society fractured by differences and dishonored tribal and cultural affiliations. For many of us, the absence of a solid community base creates a spiritual and social vacuum needing to be filled. This absence cries out for the creation of different kinds of rituals than the ones that functioned for my grandfather and his community. At this point in human history, there is a pressing need to integrate all the cultural, human, and natural resources to ensure our survival. Throughout my lifelong search for dances of deep devotion, I have discovered road maps that have helped many communities. By exploring how we can make dance rituals to facilitate community process, I have learned that many challenging life experiences can be confronted through dance. Some specific ones might be AIDS, child abuse, homelessness, isolation, violence, environmental destruction, racism, death, marriage, initiation, or celebration. It is my intention in this book to present a philosophy and a process that can be used to create dance rituals that apply to any important theme facing you, your community, and our world.

As we confront specific issues in our creation of embodied rituals, we gain a window into the larger, mythic polarities of life and death, male and female, good and evil, culture and nature, self and other. In dances of this sort, it is important to take a leap of faith from the specifics of the situation and look at its larger ramifications. When, for example, we confronted the AIDS epidemic in *Circle the Earth: Dancing with Life on the Line* (see chapter 3), we also touched on a variety of bigger contexts: the struggle around life and death, the destruction of the environment, the limitations of human resiliency, the chaos and unraveling of the twentieth century, and the power of nature over culture. As we learn to reweave our personal experiences into the fabric of the larger human experience, we turn a story into a "myth" and a dance into a "ritual." Just as the astronaut's first look at the earth from the moon became a symbol for human unity, so too the human body in *Circle the Earth: Dancing with Life on the Line* becomes a symbol of our connection to one another. If one of us has AIDS, we are all ill. The personal body is a fractal of the communal body, each reflecting the other. When we dance from that kind of wisdom we expect the healing of the personal body and the collective body to arise reciprocally.

I have struggled for years to find a name for this approach to dance. I have chosen the words "myth" and "ritual," even though there are certain problems inherent in doing so. For the purpose of this book, "myth" is defined as a series of symbols, actions, and stories that, when placed together in a certain order, create meaning and give significance to our individual and collective experience. A myth is not a fantasy or an untruth. It is a story we discover in our bodies, and it is both unique and common to us all. When expressed in words, a myth is a story; in sound, it becomes music; in visual images, a painting or sculpture; through the shaping of matter, myth becomes a dwelling, a village, a temple, a garden, or an altar; and through physical movement, a dance or drama. The term "ritual" refers to the enactment or performance of the myth, and either everyone participates or some perform while others witness it. Witnesses are different from audience members in that they have an active supporting role in the ritual; audience members observe a performance with a less conscious intention and empathize in a more passive way. Audience members want to be entertained; witnesses want to participate. In ritual theater, the audience is part of the performance; for this reason, I refer to them as witnesses.

All the myth-making rituals I've worked with aim to answer some fundamental questions: Who am I and where do I belong? What do I value? Who are we as a community? What is our collective identity? How can we accept our differences and find our commonalities? What is our connection to the mystery of creation? What are our attitudes about life and death? What spiritual values do we embrace? These are fundamental human concerns expressing themselves over time and place; it is remarkable how community-based dance creates an opportunity for us to learn more deeply about ourselves in relation to one another and to the wider world. Our myths identify and tap into our deeper need to take part in the mystery of life.

Although there are underlying principles governing the rituals of traditional cultures, we cannot borrow or imitate them. We can bow to the enduring power of dance ritual that our ancestors knew in their bones, but we must return to the narratives that are really our own—living in our own bodies, speaking about our own experiences—to forge a new way of honoring our human dignity. The challenge and excitement of making contemporary rituals lie in discovering and exploring what is relevant, necessary, and alive for us *today*. I am interested in what emerges from our present personal and collective experiences, as opposed to borrowing from other cultures and traditions outside our experience. It is our task to discover who we are as individuals and who we are in relation to earth and one another. We live in a changing world, where traditional structures are falling away. Yet, as humans, we hunger for rituals to mark the pivotal experiences of our lives. Our need to make sense and meaning out of our lives is perhaps the thing that is most specifically human, empowering us in the task of responding to the randomness of experience.

This book reveals how, when we personalize a universal experience such as living or dying and translate it into dance, the "dancing" of this experience can transform our lives. This goes beyond simply presenting real-life issues as performative images and moves into the realm of creating dance experiences that have the potential to change the dancer. A contemporary dance ritual should address the needs of the participants and attend to each individual's personal story as well as to the universal problem the myth addresses. Encompassing diversity is one of the challenges in making this kind of ritual. We are a culture of many people from many places, and we often do not know how to bridge the distances between us. A contemporary ritual that speaks to our differences will encompass this diversity *and* place an equal value on everyone's story. A contemporary ritual that speaks to our differences will acknowledge our individual responses to the universal problems facing us. In political terms, ignoring individual input and fabricating a collective view is coercive and dangerous. In ecological terms, privileging one kind of awareness to the exclusion of another creates a monoculture, which is unsustainable over time. It's too late in the history of the world to dismiss the contributions of every individual to the strength of the whole. If we are to rebuild our culture, we must learn, experientially, how each individual story weaves into and strengthens the fabric of our collective body.

I believe we can create new dance rituals at this juncture between the individual and the collective body. But it doesn't work to start from preconceived ideas or concepts of who we are and what rituals we think we need. We need to work with the essential language of the body and movement, a language that hasn't been shaped so specifically by our censoring minds. This will show us what we really need, not what we think we need.

At the heart of this book are accounts of two dances: the *Planetary Dance*, which continues to be performed in different communities throughout the world, and *Circle the Earth: Dancing with Life on the Line*, which evolved from a series of community dances and affirmed that, after years of searching, my collaborators and I had found a path toward a dance that mattered. For many years I had been asking these questions: Can dance be used as an effective tool in healing social divisions? Can dance reveal myths and enable us to enact purposeful rituals? Can dance be for everyone and still be art? Can we find ways to sustain our search for our own myths and rituals? Can dance once again be a participatory and creative act of an entire community, an integrated part of its life? With the evolution of these two dances, I offer an enthusiastic "Yes!"

Today there is a large community of dance artists who are exploring how to create dances that catalyze social change. This book offers just one perspective among many possibilities. It is about all that I have discovered so far, about the different ways I have learned to release the secrets of the body and create individual and collective dances that evoke emotions and images. These are dances that facilitate change, dances that matter. It describes how I have worked to create a cultural, social, and artistic form to shape a dance of necessity. Both *Circle the Earth* and its offshoot, the widely performed *Planetary Dance*, provide an opportunity for people to come together over issues of great concern and to communicate across the borders that may separate us in our ordinary lives.

The Life/Art Process

An Approach to Making Dances That Matter

I

Over the many years of my career, I have evolved a series of maps to outline the territory my dances traverse. They are all rooted in a search for meaningful movement connected to somatic experiences, emotions, and our encounter with the environment. Over time, the processes I have worked with have evolved into multistep "instructions," which can be applied by anyone wanting to create dances and rituals with community groups. Because these instructions derive their power from our individual and collective life experiences, and an inquiry into how to transform them, I call this approach the Life/Art Process.

The Life/Art Process is a theoretical framework for dances like *Circle the Earth: Dancing with Life on the Line*, the dance detailed in chapter 3.[1] This process is based on the notion that movement, sensations, emotions, and images are interactive and that cultivating and exploring the interactions between them allows participants to connect with an authentic experience, free from their preconceived ideas about "Art." Through this process, people have an opportunity to experience what is real for them, and the expression of this authentic experience is their art. This method stresses differences in human experience and individual expression, while acknowledging the inherent biological and psychological characteristics common to all human beings. The Life/Art Process therefore supports diversity as well as commonality. The process encourages exploration and experimentation, and generates new and effective responses to life situations. Through it, people can creatively identify life concerns, resolve conflicts, and support integration, both personally and within a larger context.[2]

The evolution of the Life/Art Process reflects the development of my work in the dance field, from comic dancer to theater artist to someone who strives to make dances that matter to the people who dance them. As I began to incorporate real-life situations into my work, I moved from making small personal and interpersonal pieces mostly designed for the theater, to pieces that focused on larger social issues and took place in venues outside the theater. One of my most important projects in developing the Life/Art Process explored the issue of racism. After the shock and horror of the Watts riots in 1965, I launched a project with an all-black group of ten dancers from Watts, Los Angeles, and an all-white group of ten from San Francisco. Culturally, there was tension in the air, emotions were running high, the risks were great, and it was clear that we needed a new way to communicate with one another across racial lines. By creating a situation where members of these two groups had to reach out and listen to one another, we placed ourselves in a microcosm of the larger social context. There was no escaping the cultural portent of the process.

The two groups worked separately on the same "scores" for nine months (see "The RSVP Cycles" later in this chapter for an explanation of scoring). I traveled to Watts every Saturday to work with the African American group, and during the week I worked with the white group. After working this way for nine months, the two groups came together in San Francisco and, using our real-life situations, we built a dance to confront our prejudices and learn from our differences. It was a difficult, challenging process. There were times that seemed like open warfare. We fought, struggled, cried, laughed, loved, and cared for one another. We evolved a piece called *Ceremony of Us* and performed it at the Mark Taper Forum in Los Angeles. It was a miraculous experiment in human contact, difference, and confrontation. In retrospect, I believe this piece was about our desperate need and struggle to survive and to learn to love the "other" as ourselves.[3]

This experience demonstrated to me that if my purpose in theater and dance was to deal with individual experience, with what was really going on in people's lives, I was going to be dealing with monsters and passion and fear, and I needed some solid and trustworthy ways to get there. I began a more conscious search for new techniques. Not the kind of physical techniques that would enable us to lift our legs higher, turn faster, fall and rebound more smoothly, or invent more dance "moves." Instead, I was looking for techniques that would include emotional, visual, theatrical, and kinesthetic experience and offer new ways to explore human nature, individually and collectively. These new techniques needed to maximize differences and commonalities, as well as allow for mutual creation and the integration of body, mind, and emotion. I wanted new ways to listen to emotions through movement and for collaborating with other artists and interfacing with the environment.

Ceremony of Us workshop, 1965. Photographer unknown. Anna Halprin Papers; courtesy of Museum of Performance and Design, San Francisco.

A few guidelines arose from my search for a dance that would meet human needs on so many different levels. The underlying principle is that *as life experiences deepen, art expression expands*, and vice versa: *as art expression deepens, life experiences expand*. This idea, when applied to groups of people, is centered around six intentions:

1. **Maximize participation.** This approach is open to all people. No formal dance training is required. All movements are potentially dance, and we are all dancers.
2. **Encourage diversity**. Honoring the differences in human experience, respecting individual expression, and encouraging cultural and ethnic input are essential.

Ceremony of Us workshop, 1965. Photographer unknown. Anna Halprin Papers; courtesy of Museum of Performance and Design, San Francisco.

3. **Search for commonality**. Despite our cultural differences, there are inherent biological characteristics common to us all as human beings—physically, emotionally, mentally, and spiritually. This creates the basis for a shared language of expression.

4. **Generate creativity**. A high value is given to involvement, experimentation, and exploration leading to the discovery of new and effective ways to respond to life situations. The process is free of judgmental reactions or an attachment to a preconceived outcome.

5. **Encourage life change, growth, and healing**. Criteria for success are based on the impact of the work in your life, the lives of others, and the environment surrounding you.

6. Develop aesthetic standards. This is achieved when a balance is struck between life experience and art expression.

Expressing your experience while experiencing your expression, moving your senses while sensing your movement—that is what makes any life movement a dance. That is living your life "art"-fully.

ORDINARY MOVEMENT

A fundamental tenet of the Life/Art Process is that we begin with the common language of movement. Everyone has a body and every body moves. None of us has to be taught how to move because we are all already moving. The language of movement is our most fluent tongue and a language all human beings hold in common. This is the key to its power to communicate, create relationships, evoke emotion, and influence our experience. For many cultural, religious, and moralistic reasons, many people today, especially in white Western culture, have shut down the full range of sensation, motion, and emotion. We emphasize sight and hearing almost to the exclusion of our other senses, especially the kinesthetic sense, but the totality of what we know comes to us through all of our senses, not just our eyes and ears. As we devalue our senses, we diminish what we know and can possibly know about one another, the world, and ourselves. We abandon our capacity to fully experience ourselves and the world in which we live.

Because many of us live at such a distance from our bodies, the use of ordinary, intrinsic movement is at the core of my approach to dance. I am committed to reconnecting people to their dancing bodies, even if they have no identification with being a dancer. I want a dance that *any body* can do—young or old, able-bodied or disabled, trained or untrained. This means the most efficient language for dance is pedestrian, common, quotidian movement. Despite how we have been culturally conditioned to ignore the signals of our bodily wisdom, we nonetheless live in our bodies every day and rely on them to participate in every aspect of our lives. So in referring to "ordinary movement," I literally mean the movements that make up the tasks we do every day: the way we walk, sit, stand, and run. The way we pick things up and put them down, the way we hold a child, the way we relax, the way we lift and drop, the way we wash the dishes. The ways we encounter one another—our voices, our songs, and our simple caresses—also are included in my dance vocabulary. We often move without thinking, yet everything we know and have experienced is reflected in the movement of our bodies. Ordinary movements of the body structure our experiences and our expression. And this kind of movement belongs to all of us, regardless of our political beliefs, our racial or religious heritage, even our individual lived experiences. This commonality is perhaps the most open-ended opportunity for us to meet across the social barriers that so often constrain our human interactions.

When we open ourselves up to all of our senses and learn to listen to what our bodies are telling us, we often find ourselves at odds with dominant cultural injunctions against feeling and responding authentically. Reclaiming ordinary movement as something important and meaningful is a resistance to routine disregard of the body. Working with people using dance to express issues that are central to us brings us quickly to a place of commonality, empowerment, and the possibility of transformation. Activating the kinesthetic sense and experiencing our bodies as resources, rather than liabilities, can help move us across outdated social boundaries that limit our compassion and our love. We can reinhabit the whole body, and in so doing, gain a dimension of understanding, creativity, and connection to the mystery of the universe that is unavailable to us when we try to understand our lives only through mental analysis.

AWARENESS OF YOUR EMBODIED SELF

I think of "the body" as a multilayered energetic form, comprised of the physical, emotional, mental, and spiritual bodies. The patterns of the body reflect and influence all the patterns of our lives. The *physical body* is the material aspect of the form—muscles, bones, tendons, blood. It is the site of sensation, and an awareness of this body gives us a continual experience of intrinsic motion. We can experience the physical body in the pulse of our blood and the wave of our breath, in our locomotor movements, and in the physical tasks we do. An awareness that we are constantly in motion is available to all of us and is at the root of what I call "dance." As we explore and work with task-oriented, natural movements to create a common language for the physical body, we are deepening our capacity to feel what our bodies naturally do: breathe, pulse, flow, stop, start, and so on.

The *emotional body* is that part of us which responds with anger, happiness, sadness, concern, empathy, or any other emotion. There is a feedback process between physical movement and emotion that both illuminates and motivates our bodies. The emotional body is not separate from the physical body, but its responses are different. Emotions form a particularly human language and need to be understood on their own terms. This can often be read on the surface of our bodies. For example, a tightly contracted, pounding fist might give rise to anger, while a softly contracted chest might generate sadness. If you change the movement to

I draw a distinction between feelings and emotions. The word "feeling" refers to a physical sensation and our awareness of it. The word "emotion" refers to our reactions to our experience and our mental associations with it. So the "feeling" of a particular movement might be of contraction while the emotion might be "scared." Or the sensation of a gentle touch may give rise to the emotion of being loved and cared for. Being able to distinguish between feelings and emotions increases our somatic literacy and helps us know ourselves that much better.

a tensely contracted chest, your emotion might change to fear. Try throwing your arms into the air with an expanded and open chest and say, "I am so depressed." It's incongruent. There is a profound relationship between how we move and the emotions we feel. This indivisible relationship forms the common language of the emotional body. I have found that working with simple instructions that direct dancers to the connection between movement and emotions helps deepen our capacity to feel our emotional versatility and range.

When we work with movement and emotions, associations and images inevitably arise. These images, associations, and thoughts arise through the actions of the *mental body*. In my workshops, we take time to draw these images and create stories from them. The content—the meaning—of our movement surfaces in these drawings and provides us with an externalized reflection of our subjective experience. This is one way we turn our experience into something we might commonly call "art." Visualizations form a common language of the mental body. We reflect, write, and share the meaning of our drawings with one another, and this level of communication makes us more visible to one another and to ourselves. This method, called the *Psychokinetic Visualization Process*, is one way to articulate the mental body without losing connection to the nonverbal nature of movement. (See "The Psychokinetic Visualization Process and Healing Through Dance" later in this chapter.)

The *spiritual body* is the most mysterious body of all, and it may be that the spiritual body always exists beyond the reach of words to describe it. It is the body that is endowed with the capacity to experience our connections to each other and the natural world. It is the body that is not only aware of the mystery of existence, but is most completely *part* of it. The spiritual body is, in one profound sense, our constant, fluctuating relationship to the life force. My deep commitment to dance stems from its ability to place me more consciously in touch with feelings of love, compassion, and the timelessness of being—the spiritual aspects of my self.

WHEN ORDINARY MOVEMENT BECOMES DANCE

What is the connection between ordinary, everyday movement and "dance"? How do we make the shift from one to the other? I believe this shift happens when we choose our movement for reasons other than the purely functional. When our awareness is focused on the expressive qualities of movement, we begin to experience it as dance. This awareness is available to anyone, regardless of any specific movement training. Dance, in these terms, is about intention, and not about the specific movements or actions themselves. Deep breathing can be a dance if we come to it with a quality of awareness and curiosity. Setting the table or sweeping the floor can be a dance. Imagine the possibilities for invigorating our lives when we bring this kind of awareness to movements we do every day.

The "techniques" I want to impart are ones that cultivate the whole person as a dancer rather than ones that make the dancer into a physical technician. When the four main levels of awareness—physical/kinesthetic, emotional, mental, and spiritual—are equally included in the process of creative expression, a bridge is made between unconscious and conscious awareness connecting the individual's inner experience with external expression. It is because of the connections between movement, emotion, image (content), and spirit that we are able to uncover our personal stories and myths, as individuals and in community. The discovery of the personal myth and its relationship to the collective myth is the first step in creating a dance that will speak to the real-life situations and needs of the dancers and witnesses.

I want to make dances in which the movement itself is so real and direct that it will create an experience in the present that does not need to be mediated by an act of interpretation. It is not so much a matter of inventing interesting, clever, or evocative movements to access the body's inner wisdom. It is more a process of finding an ordinary movement that is essential, one that serves the intention of the dance. Reaching, stretching, backing up, turning around, running, falling, rising are all ordinary movements, but when they are selected in relation to an intention and you notice the emotions and images they evoke, they transform into an artistic expression of who you are. When done with self-awareness, these ordinary movements create a visceral response in both dancer and witness. This kind of dance is filled with meaningful movements that serve a special intent.

Try this experiment. Put your arm out in front of you with your palm facing up. Notice what emotions arise. Then twist your hand so the palm is facing forward. Notice if this evokes a different response. Another experiment: Bow your head with the image of prayer. Then bow your head with the image of shame. How is that different?

This kind of movement can be generated in two different ways. You can generate a movement and see what experience it evokes. This can be as simple as enacting the instruction "Extend your arm and hand from the shoulder blade, and notice what happens." By following this direction, you are allowing the mind to lead the body. What is important is that you are not being prescriptive about movement—you do not seek a movement to evoke a specific state. Rather, you notice what state the movement evokes.

A different approach is to just sense how your body wants to move, without any preset ideas. You don't choose the movement; the movement chooses you. Think of some of our common descriptions of movement in relation to emotion. We jump for joy. We wring our hands in grief. We stomp in anger. When emotional states are intense and images clearly defined, the appropriate movements will arise.

One of the great attributes of movement is that it is malleable. You can be guided into discovering movements you would never think of doing yourself because of all your conditioning. Our belief systems have so shaped our responses that we tend to repeat the same habitual, inhibited patterns over and over again. Yet, in a safe and trusting atmosphere, you can be guided into doing movements that are totally fresh and new, that would never have come out of your own stimulus-response patterns. These movements may not seem to match the way you think you feel, yet when you do them, they open up a whole new vocabulary, a whole new possibility in life that you didn't know was there.

When leading a workshop, I try to create the conditions for this kind of movement to arise. It's important to establish a nonjudgmental atmosphere, where people understand that nothing they do is wrong. We've been loaded down with so many shoulds and shouldn'ts that we've lost the capacity to fully experience ourselves and our truths through our bodies. I am not interested in teaching a particular style of movement; rather, I want people to get in touch with how they move naturally, without aiming for a particular effect.

My teaching involves a balancing of structure and freedom. Imagine that you've come to my studio for a class. We might begin with the physical body, with the question: Where am I in my body? Here's what I might instruct you to do: Lie down on the floor, then start to roll very slowly. To heighten your awareness, pay attention to the shapes, feelings, and sensations in your arms. Whenever I give a cue, stop and appreciate your position in space, as if you were a piece of sculpture. What emotions come up? Is there an image? Now roll the other way, this time paying attention to your head. What are the physical sensations? And what is the relationship between your head and the other parts of your body? When you move your head, what happens to your arms, for example?

Next I might focus on the ribs in relation to rolling. I make sure there are lots of pauses, so people can really appreciate the sculptural quality of their movement. In this way the class is developing resources, exploring movement possibilities and deepening their awareness. We spend a lot of time doing this, so people can really relax. The directions are simple, but they require connecting the brain to the body. I also call attention to the breath, how it is generated in the ribs and moves through the body. Dance, I believe, is breath made visible.

After the ribs we might look at the spine in relation to rolling. What happens when you move your sacrum? How does it connect to your pelvis, your legs, your arms, and your head? Now go to the lumbar region and discover how much range of movement there is. When I teach, the way I speak is important: I'm not telling people what movement to expect but asking them to explore, engaging them in the process rather than dictating, so I ask a lot of questions like, "When you do this, what do you notice?" This allows people to continue to deepen their internal awareness of sensation and emotion, rather than understanding what they are doing only through their cognitive awareness.

Now I might introduce movement dynamics, asking people to notice what happens if they start moving slowly but then shift and move quickly, then stop. Adding dynamics shapes movement in a different way. It may stimulate an emotional response. Compare, for instance, the emotional quality of a slow, flowing roll to suddenly tightening up all over. As people continue to develop their movement with dynamics, they may find themselves carried to a different level, perhaps even to standing. I encourage them to explore where the movement takes them in space.

At a point when participants seem comfortable with their own creativity and are beginning to generate their own personal responses to my simple questions, I might introduce music. Music will profoundly affect the space, often suggesting common emotions and associations. This helps facilitate our interactions with one another. I encourage these interactions with directives such as: "Notice who you are with. How might other people be influencing your movement? Notice how interacting with another person can expand your movement vocabulary. You may find yourself doing a movement you would never have thought of by yourself."

In this kind of exploration every movement that arises is part of a process of listening for what best expresses who you are and how you are feeling in that moment. I believe that our bodies hold stories about who we are, and all of us, because of our different experiences, have our own stories to tell. When we take the time to listen, without overthinking what we are doing, we open the door for our physical and emotional bodies to share their wisdom with us. We almost always discover unexpected stories that have been there all along, below the level of conscious awareness. Much has been written in recent decades about how the body holds our stories—some authors say "the body never lies"; others say "the body bears the burden" or "the body keeps the score." Research reveals that our stories live deep within our muscles and bodies, affecting our neurobiology, our relationship patterns, and our expectations for love and for strife. Isn't it time we turned to face ourselves and learned to listen?

THE POWER OF BODY WISDOM

Let me give you an example of how body wisdom can remain dormant for decades until we become open to it. One time when I was getting some bodywork done, the masseuse got right underneath my shoulder blade, and all of a sudden I started seeing a scene from my past. It was something I hadn't ever really thought about; people had told me about it, but I didn't identify with it. As a young child, I used to go every evening with Hugo, our chauffeur, to pick up my father at the station, and I would run across the street to meet him at the train. One evening I ran across the road and a car came out of nowhere and hit me. It had apparently hit me right where the masseuse touched me, evoking a memory lodged for decades in my body. I saw myself being hit by the car and dragged for half a block. The terror of that experience was something that had been totally blocked. I started screaming and then just sobbing. And then I remembered how Hugo picked me up and cared for me. It wasn't my father, it was Hugo who held me in his arms and comforted me and carried me. Why was it Hugo, and not my father? Emotions of shock and sadness, of always wanting to be held by my father, arose from this one pressure point in my body.

This story provides a good example of how an experience can live on in the body, long after that experience has occurred. Talking about it may not fully clear trauma—it often needs to be processed on a kinesthe-

As my daughter Daria Halprin has written: "The entire repertoire of our life experiences can be accessed and activated through the body in movement. Since movement is the primary language of the body, moving brings us to deep feelings and memories .... Whatever resides in our body—despair, confusion, fear, anger, joy—will come up when we express ourselves in movement. When made conscious, and when entered into as mindful expression, movement becomes a vehicle for insight and change."[4]

tic level. As you can see from this story, the kinesthetic sense was connected to my capacity to remember and to feel emotions about what had happened to me, even though so many decades had passed. This is what is meant by "the body bears the burden." The body is the one map you always carry with you, and it is shaped by all of your life experience, both positive and negative. As a guide and teacher, reference text and tool, it is vast and matchless. A good map may show many different ways to get where you want to go, and it will also show the way to places you've never been before. All the information we need to make a new choice, to take another road to another place, is encoded in our bodies. But we have forgotten how to really read the map. We have limited ourselves to just a part of the picture and mistaken this part for the whole. An important function of the Life/Art Process is the practice it gives us in listening to the multiple levels of meaning within our bodies, even—or especially—when hard or unpleasant memories and sensations are found there. The skill of tapping our body wisdom gives us a more complete experience of all the things that have happened to us, deeply affecting our capacity to direct our lives in the present and the future.

THE PSYCHOKINETIC VISUALIZATION PROCESS AND HEALING THROUGH DANCE

When movement is liberated from the constricting armor of stylized, preconceived gestures, an innate feedback process between movement and emotions is generated. This feedback process is an essential ingredient of expressive movement. When you understand this, movement becomes a vehicle for releasing emotions that are essential in a healing process. The feedback process operates on a level that may not be verbal. It is not always possible to express in words the content of what we feel, where our emotions are coming from, and how to work with the emotions that arise in our personal lives. In trying to understand the messages our bodies are giving us, rather than analyzing or interpreting in a cognitive way, I have found it helpful to use a technique that comes from my years of working with children. After some movement practice, I ask participants to draw the images generated in their mind's eye by their movements and emotions. These drawings, made on paper or canvas, are what I call visualizations. They are intuitive in the same way that movement is when it taps into a deep primal source. What's important is that these drawings reveal stories that we wouldn't otherwise be in touch with, much as dreams do.

Such visualizations provide an opportunity to symbolize an experience, giving you something to refer back to. A symbol may contain many layers of significance, and it remains there in front of you to contemplate, whereas movement is very immediate and fleeting—you move and it's gone. A visualization is more like a totem, a reflection. You look at it and that reconnects you with the experience, allowing you to feel the moment again. In addition, you may gain insights about what the drawing is saying to you. The process doesn't end with the drawing, however. I have discovered that it is then necessary to dance your visualization, to connect its images to your movements and emotions through dance. Once you draw an image and dance it, the visualization you create after this dance will be different from the one you did before. So the dance is changing the dancer. It is clear that through this process we can receive messages from an intelligence within our bodies that is deeper and more unpredictable than anything we can understand through rational thought. This process—the Psychokinetic Visualization Process—supports the transformation of the dancer.

These ideas have been reinforced by a personal experience with healing that influenced the creation of *Circle the Earth*. In 1972 I was diagnosed with cancer. While a cancer diagnosis is sadly not unusual these days, the circumstance of my diagnosis *was* unusual. As a dancer working from a holistic approach, I had always been concerned with the relationship between the mind and the body. I understood the connection between movement and emotion, but perceiving how the mind works in relation to the body wasn't so simple for me. At the time of my diagnosis, I was actively exploring the use of visualizations as a way of making that link between mind and body.

One day while I was participating in the Psychokinetic Visualization Process, I drew an image of myself I was unable to dance. This was a signal to me. Why couldn't I dance it? What was blocking me? I had drawn a round ball in my pelvic area. I intellectualized that it was a symbol of an embryo pointing the way to new beginnings. But some part of me was sure that this interpretation of my drawing was wrong, because I didn't want to put the drawing into motion. That night, when my mind was quiet, I had intimations that the image I had drawn had something to tell me, and that I was not listening.

The next day I made an appointment with my doctor. I asked him to examine me precisely where I had drawn this round ball. He diagnosed cancer.

I went through traditional operation procedures, and radical ones at that, altering my body for life and leaving me with feelings of real uncertainty about my future. Would I ever dance again? The doctor assured me I was just fine, which was odd because I didn't feel fine! He also added that if I didn't have a recurrence within five years, I would be totally out of the woods. Three years after my operation, I had a recurrence. I knew then that I was going to have to make some very drastic changes in my life and my art.

After my recovery from the first operation, I began intensive research. I wanted to understand how it was possible to receive an unconscious message about something in my body through a drawing. For a period of three years, I collected slides of drawings done by students in my classes and I studied them, trying to find a coherent visual language I could understand. I thought perhaps certain colors and shapes meant something or that certain symbols had a particular meaning. But if there was a system in this, I could not find it. What I did find was that none of these questions could be answered in a rational, logical, or systematic manner. It just didn't work that way for me. What seemed to work was the *process*: when people danced their images and moved back and forth between dancing and drawing, the messages would be made clear through their movements and drawings. The visual images couldn't be codified in rigid terms because each person had a unique story and expressed it in a personal way.

At the same time, certain symbols and principles seemed to repeat themselves. For example, in a whole classroom of self-portraits, which often took weeks to create, I might notice that almost every drawing had a snake or a tree or a water image. Or that the drawings indicated polarities and opposites—a dark side and a light side. In conjunction with the intense individuality of each drawing, certain common themes seemed to appear again and again. I learned that until these images were personally experienced through dance and movement, their messages remained mysterious. It became apparent how some of the repeating images and polarities had to do with the ways we are all connected to our common environment—the natural world—and the elements that make our lives similar to one another's. This is what Jung refers to as the "collective unconscious," a collection of images that we, as human beings, share. It could be that these images are lodged in the cells of our bodies and that they connect us to one another across time and across culture.

Let me describe how I learned something about my life story, the mystery of my own personal imagery, and my connection to the natural world by dancing a self-portrait created at the time of the recurrence of my illness. When I first drew myself, I made myself look "perfect." I was young and brightly colored. My hair was blowing in the wind. I was the picture of health and vitality. When I looked at the image after drawing it, I knew I couldn't even begin to dance it; it just didn't feel like me. I turned the paper over and furiously began to draw another image of myself. It was black and angular and angry and violent. I knew that this back-side image of me was the dance I had to do. When I did it, I was overwhelmed by the release of rage and anger. I kept stabbing at myself and howling like a wounded animal. Witnesses said it sounded like I spoke in tongues. I had to have witnesses because I knew that unless I did, I would never be able to go through this ordeal. My witnesses were my family, my colleagues, and my students, and they kept me honest, urging me to go deeper, reinforcing my sounds, calling out parts of the picture I was to dance. I danced until I was spent, until I collapsed and began to sob with great relief. Now I was ready to turn the picture over and dance the healing image of myself.

As I danced this image, I imagined my breath was water and that my movements flowed through my body just as water would flow. I imagined that the water was cleansing me. I had an image of water cascading over the mountains near my home, of water flowing through me and out to the endless vastness of the sea, taking with it my illness. I believe I was experiencing the forces of nature as they are imprinted onto my body, which gave me a deep sense of the real connection between my body and the world around me. The movements of this dance started soft and small, and as I continued to dance, I added sound. My witnesses again reinforced these sounds as the movements grew and grew, until my whole body was engaged in the image of cascading water. When I finished, I invited the witnesses to join me in a circle; I felt ready to return to my friends and family.

Something happened in this dance that I can't explain. I felt I had been on a mysterious journey to an ancient world. Time and place were suspended; I was in a timeless blue void. The experience left me shaken and cleansed. Later, as I gained distance from the experience of my dance, I began to notice a pattern in it that seemed relevant to other healing processes. Much later, while developing theory and methods to apply to my teaching, I saw how this experience was the source of a healing process.

Anna dancing the light side of her 1974 cancer self-portrait. Photo by Lawrence Halprin; courtesy of Anna Halprin.

This experience gave me a new way of looking at healing, which I have used ever since as a guide to working with others and in developing my dances, including *Circle the Earth*. I have mapped out the touchstones of that journey and have found that they apply not only to my own healing, but also to the healing journey in general. These touchstones—the "Five Stages of Healing"—underlie my work with other people with life-threatening conditions in *Circle the Earth*. Admittedly, the Five Stages of Healing, like all systems, draw lines of black in places that are really gray. Healing, although it has different aspects and stages, is both more seamless and circuitous than any system can articulate fully. But I believe the Five Stages of Healing can offer guiding choreographic structures for a dance workshop and performance like *Circle the Earth: Dancing with Life on the Line* (detailed in chapter 3).

1. **Identification.** The first stage is simply to look and see and *identify* the issue, noticing the polarity between the light side and the dark side. In my personal journey, this stage was my discovery that I had cancer and realizing that the issue was whether I would live or die.

2. **Confrontation**. This stage entails the enactment of emotions and images responsive to the life-or-death issue. In my cancer experience, it involved dancing my fears, my rage, and my anguish. I had to confront the dark side of my being.

3. **Release**. After I danced my rage and fear about my illness, my body softened and relaxed, and I wept.

4. **Change**. After the release, the next step is to find a way to integrate the new changes. This stage takes place when an individual or group is ready to move to another level of awareness. It was the stage when I did the water dance in my own healing process, transforming my repressed rage into positive strength and power.

5. **Assimilation**. The final step is an assimilation of the experience into one's ongoing life. For me, this entailed a coming back to my community and my family and my life with new purpose and understanding. The learning I gained in my healing dance made it possible for me to teach and score with others using this same process. I assimilated my experience into my work and use it now to serve others.

Taken together, these Five Stages of Healing constitute a rite of passage, a series of activities marking moments of significance in a person or a community's life. Traditionally, rites of passage acknowledge the passage of time—birth, entrance into adulthood, marriage, and death are all marked by rites of passage. In the Jewish culture, for example, a bar or bat mitzvah marks a child's entrance into the adult world; sitting shiva with family and friends to mark the death of a loved one is another rite of passage. There is a strong human urge to mark these moments, both as individuals and within the context of community. My self-portrait and my dance served as a personal rite of passage; *Circle the Earth* and the *Planetary Dance* offer rites of passage for an entire community.

I become so excited by the discoveries of the visualization process and the road map for a healing journey that I often forget to tell people that, after doing my healing dance with my family and friends, my cancer went into remission. I don't say that I was cured. A cure is an event, neither predictable nor always available. The process of healing interests me more, because healing is available to all of us, all the time. I am not discounting the importance of doctors' interventions, but I believe healing also involves our attitudes toward our bodies and our illnesses, our willingness to challenge our values and lifestyles and points of view.

Changing our relationship to illness has to do with changing our relationship to our experience of living and dying. When we approach healing as an ongoing dialogue with our body and our mortality, surrender to what is beyond our control, and grasp an understanding of the power we have in our own living and dying, I believe our relationship to healing, and death, will change. The creation of *Circle the Earth* is grounded in the belief that the process of the dance is as relevant as its outcome, just as the process of illness is as relevant as its outcome.

THE RSVP CYCLES

In developing a community ritual like *Circle the Earth*, we are asking people to share very personal, deep-seated concerns and emotions; we are asking them to expose themselves. So it is critical to have a process that feels safe and clear. An integral component of this process is a method of collective creativity called the RSVP Cycles, which my husband, Lawrence Halprin, developed and which I began using with dancers in the early 1970s.[5] This method welcomes and incorporates the personal stories of each participant. The core of the RSVP Cycles lies in the separation of the four elements of creativity.

> *R* stands for *Resources.* These are the basic materials we have at our disposal, including not only physical resources but also human ones, encompassing movement possibilities, mental imagery, emotions, motivations, aims, and more.

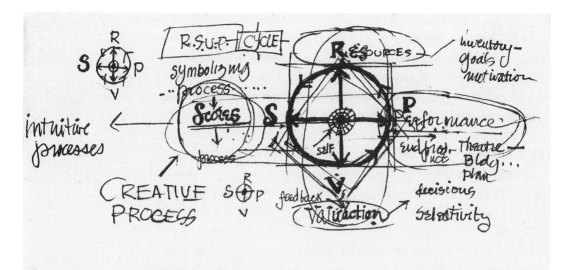

Drawing of RSVP
Cycle by Lawrence
Halprin. Courtesy of
Anna Halprin.

S stands for *Scores.* The word "score" is derived from music and
refers to a visual and/or verbal plan that instructs a group of
people to carry out prescribed activities to fulfill a particular
intention. In addition to the activities, a score delineates place,
time, space, and the cast of people, as well as sound and other
related elements. It guides performers in what to do, who
does it, when to do it, and where to do it. To varying degrees,
it may indicate how to do the activities, but this can range from
being very closed (with all the actions precisely defined, leaving
little room for improvisation) to being very open (emphasizing
improvisation and exploration).

V stands for *Valuaction.* This coined term is short for "the value of
the action" and allows for analysis, appreciation, feedback, value-
building, and decision-making to accompany the process of
creation.

P stands for *Performance.* This is, quite simply, the enactment of
the score.

These four component parts of the RSVP Cycles are not connected in a
linear way. Once a cycle begins, the development of a dance might move
from performance to valuaction to a new score to valuaction to gathering resources and so on, back and forth. My method is to use a workshop
setting to provide opportunities for participants to discover their own resources, thereby ensuring that the performance that evolves will be both
a personal and a collective one. The RSVP Cycles are a highly responsive structure encouraging creative participation at all levels. Exploring

resources can help performers discover greater personal meaning in the activities they do in performance. If our concern is how to connect movement to emotion, we might try a contractive movement and explore how it makes us feel emotionally. We might try that movement with a lot of intensity and see what arises. Fear? Anxiety? When we then move with less intensity, we have a different experience. Using our sensations, we can expand our resources in movement. As a workshop leader, if you want your participants to be able to express a range of emotions through movement, you need to help them develop a vocabulary they can draw from by experimenting with different values, intensity, and duration in movement.

One of my "tests" for a good score is: Does it generate creativity in the performers? A simple score might be: "Everyone go to the other side of the space now." It tells who (everybody), what (go), where (other side), and when (now). But in this score, "how" is completely undefined. The movement options open to performers are endless—walk, run, crawl, spin, go quickly or slowly. Other choices include going across directly, on a diagonal, and so on. If I wanted to make a score extremely open, I might say: "Do whatever you want whenever and however you want." This kind of score encourages improvisational spontaneity, but too much freedom can be as paralyzing to creativity as too little. A very closed score might be the choreography for a ballet, where there are precise models for the performance of each step. My scores generally fall in between these two extremes.

The scores for the community rituals detailed in this book are open enough to allow different individuals and groups to embody them in unique ways, so the culminating performance will never be exactly the same. The diversity of the performers, the dynamics of the group, and any cultural differences that exist will all affect how a score is performed. Although the score provides an overall framework, it does not exclude new input and change. Instead, it promotes creativity and growth. A score is like a living thing, constantly shaped by our experience. The image of a tree comes to mind: it remains a tree in essence even as it responds to such forces as wind, rain, and sun.

People sometimes ask how closely participants need to follow the score, how committed to it they need to be. What happens if they "break" the score, if they take an element of the score that's closed and open it? If you feel that an important aspect of the score is being lost, you may want to step in and gently remind participants of the score by modeling the activity it calls for, as I sometimes do when participants stray from a unifying drumbeat. At times people break a score because they don't understand it or aren't clear about its purpose. Some people may break a score

The score for the *Planetary Dance* (see chapter 4) calls on participants to declare what they are dancing for in relation to peace among peoples and with the earth. Someone once said to me that she needed to dance for her own needs. This might be a fine intent for a different score, but the *Planetary Dance* score instructs people to dance for the needs of others. One challenge for *Planetary Dance* leaders is how to help people hone their focus within the score. Often people say they intend to dance for "love." My response to this is always to ask for more specificity. What do you love? Take the mirror away from yourself and show it to the world around you.

because they're feeling rebellious or bored. Still others may believe that, because the score doesn't match their emotions, they can't do it. Part of one's role in presenting a score is to understand the score well enough to communicate it to others, to help them embody it.

In workshops like the one detailed in chapter 3, we don't do scores because they match our emotions. We do scores to see what emotions they will evoke. If you come to one of my workshops, I would ask you to commit to the scores of the workshop, to give yourself to the scores without preconceptions of how they will make you feel. At one point we may be doing a score of celebration, and you may feel angry, sad, tired, or depressed. You may not want to have anything to do with anyone. The challenge, then, is to find a way to follow the score and see what emotions it brings up. What is it like to stay within a score when your mood is in a completely different place from everyone else's? That's the challenge—to stay within the score, not to break it. Really committing to a score is one way to get the most out of it.

Another thing that can interfere with getting the most out of a score is closing a previously open element. Especially in the beginning of a workshop, I use scores in which the intention is to explore, research, find out different possibilities, so closing parts of the score that are open will close down innovation and avenues of discovery. A simple score might ask you to investigate rising and falling movements. If you start out with a strong idea of what rising and falling are about, you will limit yourself. There could be more than a hundred different ways of rising and falling, so if you restrict yourself to one idea in the beginning, you're closing a part of the score that's open and you won't get the most value from it. So when a score is open, be mindful about making choices that close it down.

Open scores give us a chance to express our differences, while closed scores help us express our commonalities. Most scores have both open and closed elements. When you have a sequence of scores over the course of a workshop or a dance, it's important to have a balance, with some scores more open and some more closed. In our culture we place a high value on individualism, so we often need to express our differences first, to know that we are honored and recognized for who we are. As modern people tempered in the forge of individuality, we seem to need to find our own personal content before we can make a commitment to our commonalities.

It's important to remember that scores can (and should) evolve. That's where *valuaction* plays a critical role. Valuaction allows people to share their experiences. It is a way of analyzing the score and its enactment to help a group make decisions and selections regarding the material and the creation of a final performance. Making this creative process visible and encouraging the input of the participants fosters mutual involvement, support, and enthusiasm. Valuactions tell us what works and what doesn't according to the core intention of the dance. This process facilitates redesigning and recycling aspects of the score to more clearly meet its intentions. Through valuactions, an ongoing process of growth and change can occur.

In the kind of community ritual described in chapter 3, the final *performance* is a presentation of the group's experience as it happens before invited witnesses (our audience). Unlike in ballet or other strictly choreographed dance forms, we are not performing a "known" experience or set of steps. In contrast to open improvisation, which is often done without concern for its effect, we dance with the specific intention to create change. The kind of performance described in this book is about bringing as much of our real lives onto the stage as possible and being witnessed in that act. There is something magical about performing, and being witnessed by other people has a focalizing effect. This magical boost offers each of us the chance to stretch beyond our ordinary limits. This performance is predicated on the belief that the expression of our experience connects us with others and that this connection helps to create a community with the collective power to enact change.

One of the greatest benefits of using the RSVP Cycles is the completely positive, nonjudgmental attitude inherent in its process. We give feedback (or valuactions) along the lines of the score; we have either completed the objectives of the score or we haven't. There is no blame. If we find we haven't met the score's objectives, we can ask questions about what happened and why. The process provides for recycling the best ideas and composting the ones that have no place in the dance. There is no hidden or higher authority dictating the way. All participants are involved in the creation of the culminating performance.

⤳ Over the course of seventy years in dance, I have honed some simple and direct approaches to movement by focusing on embodied awareness, ordinary movement, how ordinary movement becomes dance, and the power of embodied wisdom. In my search for living myths and rituals, I have evolved powerful processes for helping groups of people make dances that make a difference. These are the Life/Art Process, the Psychokinetic Visualization Process, the Five Stages of Healing, and the RSVP Cycles. All of these processes provide maps to the territory of the self; they help us make authentic art expressions derived from real life experience. To more clearly illuminate these maps and the scoring process that gives rise to individual expression around common themes and enables groups of people to focus their concern and care around issues that matter to them, this book focuses on two community rituals: *Circle the Earth: Dancing with Life on the Line* and the *Planetary Dance*. But before entering into in-depth descriptions, I'd like to recount briefly how these dances evolved.

A History of *Circle the Earth* and the *Planetary Dance*

2

Circle the Earth and the *Planetary Dance* have two histories: a long one and a short one. The long story begins in the 1950s. At that time I was researching ways for individuals and groups to tap into their personal and group mythologies through dance and movement. Later, in the sixties and seventies, I created group events that enabled people to invent their own stories rather than sitting back and watching mine. It was important for me to use dance as a way to help people connect with their own experiences and their own sense of power. I focused on inventing ways for each individual to access his or her personal mythology. Out of these experiments and explorations, a series of road maps, a technology of methods, evolved.[6]

Until then, I had used some of that technology with specific groups, but never really had the opportunity to amplify this personal process to a community level. My 1969 dance *Ceremony of Us*, which focused on racism, was confrontational, raw, and challenging, both for us as individuals and for our audience. Throughout the process, I felt the potential for causing harm when addressing hot topics like racism without a strong road map. An objective process for working with groups of people was needed if we were actually going to deal with issues that mattered. I started practicing ways to apply what I knew about dance to people's real-life experiences and to do this for larger and more diverse communities.

It is against the backdrop of these previous explorations with people's direct experiences, and their individual experience in relation to the collective, that the story of *Circle the Earth* begins. My husband, Lawrence Halprin, a landscape architect and urban designer, had been working with groups of people around issues of community development in relation to the environment using the RSVP Cycles. I found that this process could be transferred to movement experiences, enabling participants to infuse a dance with emotions and images connected directly to their own stories. My husband and I were curious to know if these processes, which we had been using in our respective fields, could be applied to entire communities to help them identify meaningful stories or "myths" related to their lives. In 1980 we envisioned a series of workshops called "A Search for Living Myths and Rituals through Dance and the Environment" and invited people to join us in an exploration of relationships to each other, our surroundings, and ourselves. We wanted people of different backgrounds and ages to have a chance to interact and become familiar with one another through movement, dance, and the environment. The series was set up as a search for a myth with a community vision. We offered free workshops in the gymnasium of the local college in our town. "A Search for Living Myths and Rituals" was planned as a series of dance and environmental workshops over nine months, culminating in a performance.

We believed that movement, art, and nature could provide focal points for a community's activities and wanted to experiment with how these elements could serve in the creation of a collective story. Everything developed intrinsically from the medium of the art experience and our experience of the natural world. We didn't start out trying to solve problems. That came later, once we had evolved a common language and a way of working together. We did this by gathering and defining the physical and imagistic symbols from our dances, our drawings, our environmental-awareness walks and studies, and our dialogues with one another.

At the time of the workshop, four women had been murdered on the trails of Mount Tamalpais, a beautiful mountain in the center of our community, and the bodies of three more women and a man had been found in nearby Point Reyes. The "Trailside Killer" was still at large, and Mount Tamalpais was no longer considered a safe place; its trails and campgrounds had been closed because of the killings. As the workshop progressed, the image of the mountain kept reappearing in people's drawings, and by the end of the series we realized that the story of the Trailside Killer and the mountain was the present-time myth of our community. We uncovered our need to reclaim the mountain and cleanse it of the destructive force that was holding it—a need to reinhabit this place that was part of our experience of home.

Larry and I provided a container for the emergence of a group myth, but in the beginning we had no idea what that myth would be. And this is how it should be—a community myth is seldom determined by only two members, and never by two members who risk taking on a leadership role. It must evolve from interactions among the collective, from their own inner lives and connections with one another, the creative process, and the natural world that supports us.

The participants in the workshop joined with dancers from the Tamalpa Institute[7] to present a culminating series of ceremonies, events, and performances, titled *In and On the Mountain* (1981), which took place over a period of two days. The first day featured a performance at the College of Marin at the foot of Mount Tamalpais. The dance included ritual reenactments of the trailside murders, with friends and families of the slain women in the audience. A series of ceremonies and rituals lasting all night and into the next day's sunrise followed that performance. On the second day, we went up the mountain. Eighty people, including some children, braved their fear of the Trailside Killer, riding in buses to the top of the mountain. There we took part in a series of offerings at each place where a woman had been murdered. People read poems and told stories; children danced spontaneously; somebody planted a tree. We were marking these tragedies and affirming our connection to the mountain. A week after our performance, an anonymous phone call helped police locate the killer. Three weeks later, the killer was caught.

Did this community dance help to catch the killer, or was it just a coincidence? Does the collective mind and spirit have the power to bring about a change of this magnitude? It doesn't really matter who gets credit for catching the killer: the dance, the mountain, the police, or the spirit. *In and On the Mountain* was a prayer, a prayer said not with words alone, but by the whole body of the collective through dance. When you say a prayer and your prayers are answered, that's not the time to start questioning whether or how prayer works. When your prayers are answered, that's the time to give thanks. And pray again.

In that spirit of gratitude and awe, the next year we created another dance, an offering of thanks that the killings had stopped and that the mountain had been reclaimed. We called it simply *Thanksgiving.* We had built a sense of community and felt we had begun to uncover a myth with both an immediate, personal meaning and a larger, more universal one. On the immediate level we were reconnecting with our mountain; more broadly we were reconnecting with the environment, restoring our place in nature and our deep appreciation of the value of aligning with one another in community.

This might have been the end of the story were it not for a visit from a 107-year-old Huichol shaman, Don Jose Mitsuwa, who came to Tamalpa Institute during the following year to present a deer dance ceremony. When we told him about our previous performances on the mountain,

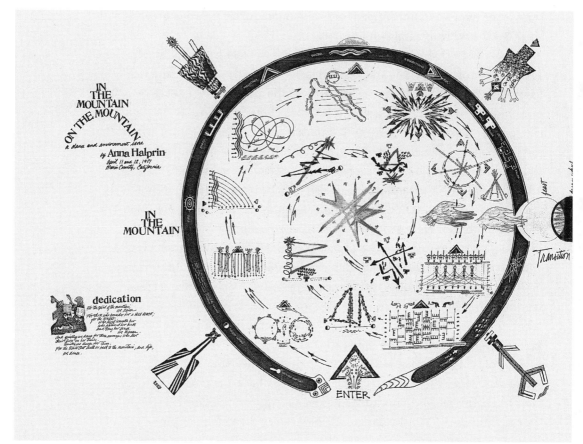

Score for *In and On the Mountain*, 1981. Anna Halprin Papers; courtesy of Museum of Performance and Design, San Francisco.

he said, "The mountain is one of the most sacred places on earth. I believe in what your community did, but to be successful in purifying this mountain, you must return to it and dance for five years." As with the Corn Dance that so moved me in Santo Domingo, New Mexico, I was confronted again with indigenous wisdom that directed us to focus our intent, ignite our enthusiasm, and repeat the motions of our dance. What had started out as an experiment had had such far-reaching results that we were committed to fulfilling Don Jose's near-directive. His words made me see that our experiment had connected to something essential. The experience had a momentum of its own, and I wanted to see where it would go and how it could integrate into the ongoing myth of my community.

By this time it was clear that one intrinsic theme of these dances was the struggle of life against death. In 1983 the dancers and participants in our workshops presented *Return to the Mountain*, in which we used images from the animal world in a dance and ceremony for peace between people and the natural environment. The next day, Don Jose joined

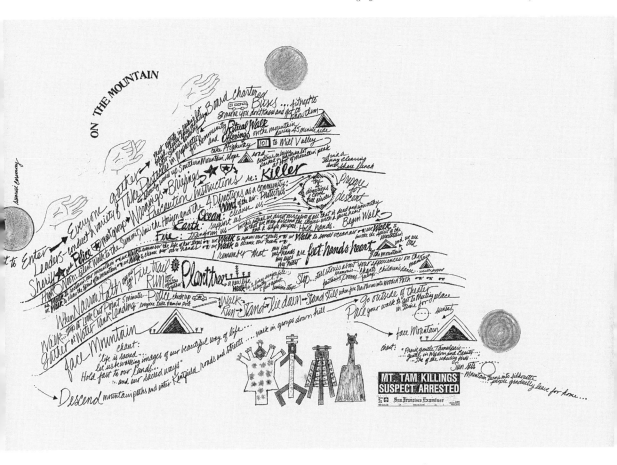

us and members of the local community for a ceremony on the top of Mount Tamalpais. He planted a feather he had received on a Himalayan peak and then led us around the top of the mountain, so we could look out and see the four directions. This moment in *Return to the Mountain* signaled a broadening of our view from our specific community needs to their connection with the larger world around us.

For the following year, 1984, we decided to use running as our theme and called our dance *Run to the Mountain*. Our intention was to dance for peace among the peoples of the world. Peace rose up as an issue of importance to us during our preparatory workshops, and we chose to highlight running because it is a movement common to all people and it symbolized the urgency of our hope for peace. A month before the performance, we began running with banners through our neighborhoods and on the Golden Gate Bridge, both to get in physical condition and to arouse curiosity about our upcoming event. The hardiest of our group ran up the mountain from four different directions. An eighty-five-year-old participant, Jack Stack, led us on the first mountain run. For many sub-

As Don Jose pointed out, Mount Tamalpais, where the dance originally took place, is historically the sacred ground of the local Miwok tribe. I wanted to honor their connection to this land as we honored our own connection to it. However, in no way was I attempting to imitate or replicate Native American rituals. I seek to honor the values of this culture, not appropriate them for my own uses.

sequent years, running continued to be an integral part of our day on the mountain.

In 1984 religious leaders from different faiths led participants around the peak, stopping in each of the four directions—north, east, south, and west—to offer inspirational words. As we made our procession, I looked out from the mountain toward the ocean and deeply felt how important it was to relate our dance not only to our mountain but to the larger world as well. At that time the greatest threat to peace on the planet was the tension between the Soviet and American superpowers and the proliferation of nuclear arms. I imagined our dance becoming a peace dance on a larger scale.

In envisioning a global scope for our dance, I realized that a local group of dancers would not be strong enough to match this vision. The power of the performance needed to match the power of the intention. I imagined one hundred people joining together to perform this dance. I thought that if enough of us danced together with a common intention it would have the potential to create change.

For our 1985 ritual, we decided to go beyond our immediate community and open the dance to anyone who wanted to perform. We sent out a call for participants: "One hundred performers to create a spirit voice strong enough so that our peaceful song is heard and our peaceful steps felt. The weapons of war have a critical mass. So, too, do the hopes of peace. We need 100 performers, 200 feet, to dance upon the planet for its life and its healing—to find a dance that inspires us to keep the earth alive." Even though one person acting alone might not make much difference, we hoped that working with a large group of people would gather more and more energy around the intention of peace and increase the possibility of creating change.

Over one hundred people came together in a high school gym, which had been transformed with banners, flowers, fruits, and special objects. I offered a weeklong workshop to ready the participants for the performance of *Circle the Mountain: A Dance in the Spirit of Peace.* We began with a run to the mountain, to gain inspiration for the dance, and then engaged in a workshop experience, preparing a performance for friends and the community. This was our fifth year of dancing in our quest to purify the mountain. Curiously, it also took exactly five years for the killer to be convicted. One cycle had ended, and another cycle begun.

I renamed the dance *Circle the Earth*, and where it was once danced to reclaim a small measure of peace on our mountain, now it was danced to reclaim peace on the planet. This is how it was described: "*Circle the Earth* is a peace dance. Not a dance about peace, not a dance for peace, but a peace dance: a dance in the spirit of peace. It is a dance that embodies our fears of death and destruction, a dance that becomes a bridge and then crosses over into the dynamic state of being called peace. *Circle the Earth* is a dance of peacemakers. A dance that makes peace within itself, makes peace with the earth on which it moves. In a world where war has become a national science, peacemaking must become a community art in the deepest sense of the word: an exemplification of our ability to cooperate in creation, an expression of our best collective aspirations, and a powerful act of magic."

As with *Circle the Mountain*, *Circle the Earth* evolved from an intensive workshop process, involving movement and sound exercises, along with drawn visualizations. Although I had already developed an overall series of scores for the culminating performance, the workshop allowed the performers to find their own responses to these scores and bring their personal experiences to bear on the final creation. The nine performance scores had evolved out of my own healing process with cancer as well as years of observing participants in very open scores and noting which results were repeated over and over. Essentially, the dance progresses from starting alone to joining another person in relationship and eventually forming a group. Once we get a feeling for our own strength and the strength of the community, we are able to look at our dark side and take on the most challenging issues of our lives. Out of that effort, which inevitably entails an expression of fear and anger, comes a release, tears, and, with comforting help from others, peace. Then, we are ready to connect with the world and send this message out.

Requests began coming in to do the dance in places other than my local community. The dance and its living myth started to travel, first to other sites in California, and then across North America to the United Nations Plaza in New York City. Using the structure developed for Mount Tamalpais, different people performed the dance in their own communities. In 1986 *Circle the Earth* crossed the Atlantic to Europe and the Pacific to Australia. By 1987 queries were arriving from interested parties

Confronting the dark side in Monster Dance from 1985 *Circle the Earth*. Photo © Paul Fusco/ Magnum Photos.

worldwide. Although it wasn't possible for me to travel to all of these places to create *Circle the Earth*, it did occur to me and to one of my Swiss students that the Earth Run, a section of the dance that we do each year on Mount Tamalpais, was a simple score that many people could adapt to their own community, no matter where they lived. If each community were to frame that dance with their own symbols and add to it out of their own community needs, the Earth Run would be a dance we could all do together, no matter where we lived. As a social species, I believe we need to come together and celebrate our unity and alignment, and to connect with the larger body of our culture and our planet. We need stories that tell of our oneness and our connection with the earth. And we need hopeful stories about living in an age threatened by pollution, nuclear devastation, overpopulation, hunger, ethnic war, and disease.

The Earth Run, which is designed for people of all ages and abilities, calls on participants to run (or walk) for others and to see their actions as influencing the larger whole. The point of the run is that people dedicate themselves to the health and healing of the planetary body. Embracing the overall intention of peace, each participant announces a personal in-

Circle the Earth in Zurich, Switzerland, 1986. Photo © Lisa Schäublin. Anna Halprin Papers; courtesy of Museum of Performance and Design, San Francisco.

tention for the run—declaring, for example, "I run for Alice and all children suffering from violence in our cities," or "I run to bring Israelis and Palestinians together." Moving to the musicians' steady beat, participants run or walk in concentric circles, creating a moving mandala. Each step becomes a call for peace. When a large number of people move together in a common pulse with a clearly defined purpose, an incredible force takes over. It is a power that can renew, inspire, and heal. The dance provides a way to symbolize our commitment to peace, mobilizing people to take action in the world.

The Earth Run transports us from a place of individuation to an experience of collective oneness. The constant repetition of one beat after another, one circle after another, helps us to see our separate lives in a community context. This repetition and connection is the essential metaphor of *Circle the Earth*, a dance we perform to create peace and healing through community action. The evolution of the Earth Run recapitulates this truth. In excerpting the Earth Run from the whole of *Circle the Earth*, I intended for each community to add its own beginning and ending, thereby personalizing the dance to suit its own needs. At this time I renamed it the *Planetary Dance* and sent a letter asking former students, dancers, and participants in *Circle the Earth* to join us on April 19, 1987, wherever they lived, in this dance of peace and healing. Instructions for

April 1. 1987.

Dear Anna

I am writing, with drawings, about Circle the Earth in Japan, and send you a bill of it.

We'll perform C·T·E· by ~~our own ways~~ at three places, Chiba, Tokyo and Kyoto. The reason is too dificult for us to organize Chief Seattle Run with many people.

Please understand this.

Where, Who, and What we'll do

At Kyoto, on April 19

Edith Egloff-Greten with her child goes and performs at the mountain (very famous in Kyoto) near her house.
And She'll send you records (some pictures).

At Tokyo, on April 19 After noon

Miyako KATO, her dance group, I and the others (musician, video cameraman, children etc.) performe at the event space conect with the street.

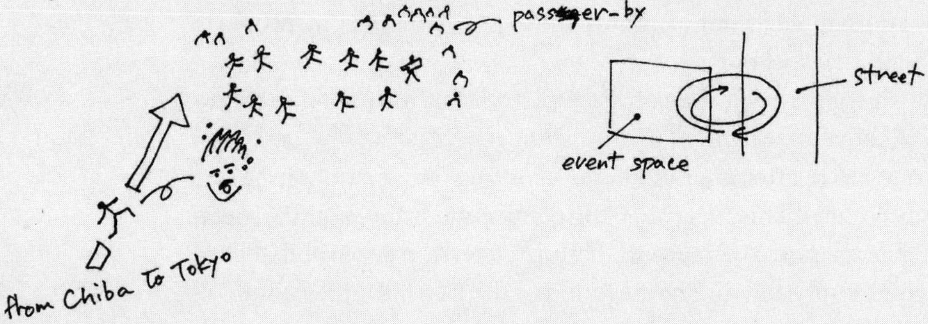

passenger-by

street

event space

from Chiba to Tokyo

Letter describing
Planetary Dance in
Japan, 1987.

At Chiba on April 18, 19

night early morning

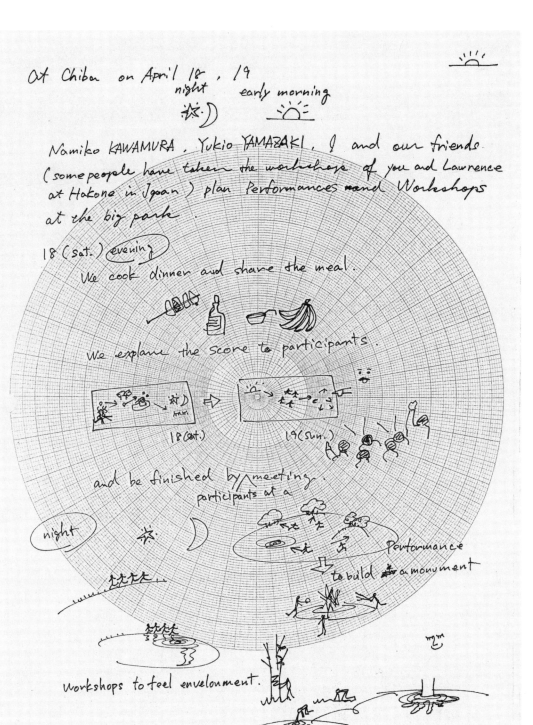

Namiko KAWAMURA, Yukio YAMAZAKI, I and our friends.
(some people have taken the workshop of you and Lawrence
at Hakone in Japan) plan Performances and Workshops
at the big park.

18 (sat.) evening
We cook dinner and share the meal.

We explane the score to participants.

18 (sat.)   19 (sun.)

and be finished by meeting.
participants at a

night

Performance
to build a monument

workshops to feel envelopment.

Planetary Dance
in Melbourne,
Australia, 1987.
Photographer
unknown.

the Earth Run were sent to interested people in communities around the world—in Switzerland, Australia, Germany, Spain, Mexico, Israel, England, Ireland, Japan, New Zealand, Indonesia, India, and many places within the United States. That year, two thousand people in thirty-seven communities performed the *Planetary Dance*, and it continues to be performed each year around the world.[8]

In 1988 we performed *Circle the Earth: Dancing Our Peaceful Nature* in an outdoor setting in the Marin Headlands. Influenced by local and world concerns, many of us began to become increasingly aware of what was happening to the environment. My attention shifted from the threat of nuclear arms to a fear for the earth herself. This was around the time of the Chernobyl devastation, when many of us were becoming more conscious of the human threat to the natural world. We decided to dance outside in an environment of sand, ocean, meadow, forest, and cliffs. The workshop participants camped in a redwood grove near the ocean. Near our campsite were military barracks from World War II, a reminder of war and the military spirit. Witnesses walked for twenty-five minutes to get to our performance site. Along the way, they could see open hillsides and the Pacific Ocean on one side, and the Golden Gate Bridge and the city of San Francisco on the other. The performance took place in a redwood grove with a giant tree at its center. The central quest of that dance was to come into a balance with the abundance of earth and the awesome technology of society.

The Planetary Dance.

a dance for peace among people and peace with the earth

Created by Anna Halprin

with James Hurd Nixon and Russell Bass

and peace-makers around the world

1981-

graphic design by Stephen Grossberg

Planetary Dance score. Graphic design by Stephen Grossberg (continued on pp. 44–45).

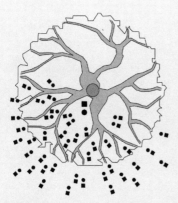

GATHERING

The community gathers around the ritual tree to receive offerings that relate to the theme of the year.

Offerings may include dance, poems, music and stories of the land.

The facilitator gives instructions for the dance with the aid of the graphic score.

TIME:
90 MINUTES

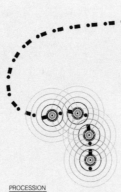

PROCESSION

The facilitator and the musicians guide the participants in single file to the site.

"Be silent and be aware of the surroundings."

TIME: 10 TO 20 MINUTES
(DEPENDING ON HOW FAR THE SITE IS FROM THE GATHERING

ENTER THE CIRCLE

If the group is large, divide into 2 parts when entering into the circle. One-half of the group goes to the left, the other to the right. Walk in a circle until the 2 groups join.

If the group is small, enter the site and divide into the four directions.

When performing the first cycle, bless the site.

The blessing of the site and the dancers are specific to each community.
TIME:
10 MINUTES

LEGEND

 STANDING DANCER

 WALKING DANCER

 MUSICIAN WALKING & PLAYING

 MUSICIANS PLAYING TOGETHER

 KNEELING DANCER

 RUNNING DANCER

 RUNNING DANCER TURNING

The Runners Rest
The facilitator signals to musicians when to bring the run to a closure.
People rest by sitting back to back and share their experiences.

SEATED DANCERS BACK TO BACK SHARING THEIR EXPERIENCE

REPEAT SYMBOL
WHEN THE MIRROR IMAGE OF THIS SYMBOL IS ENCOUNTERED RETURN TO THIS POINT.

CODA SYMBOL
THIS SYMBOL TELLS YOU TO SKIP AHEAD IN THE SCORE TO WHERE THE CODA REOCCURS.

repeat
2 times

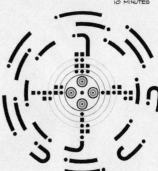

Prayer

After the third run cycle,

Everyone touches the ground and prays.

Then participants rise and blow breath through their hands into the sky.

TIME:
10 TO 15 MINUTES

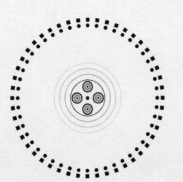

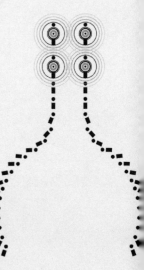

THE FIRST RUN

There are three run cycles in the planetary dance.

Before beginning the first run, each dancer will stand and make a declaration of a personal issue or cause for which they are running.

THE SECOND RUN

In the second run cycle, when their turn comes, the dancer will make a dedication for a person, place or issue in the world.

The group returns to a large circle to begin the second run.

The dancers are more aware of each other and spontaneous group interactions can emerge.

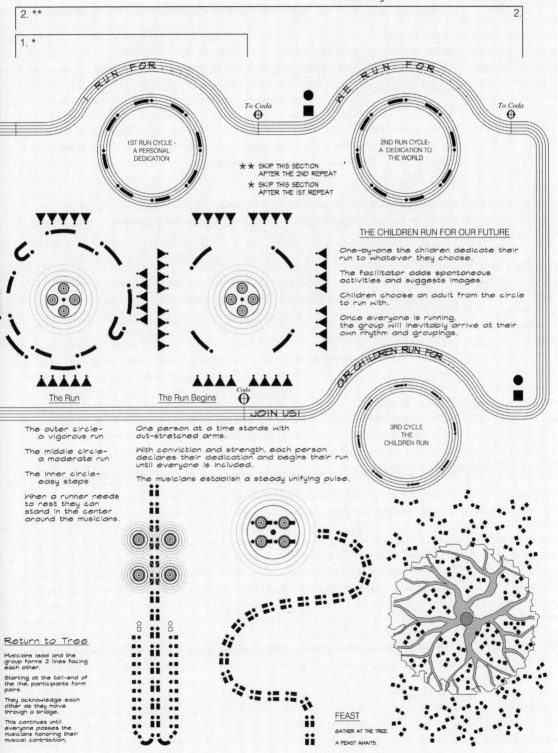

2. **

1. *

I RUN FOR

WE RUN FOR

To Coda

1ST RUN CYCLE - A PERSONAL DEDICATION

2ND RUN CYCLE - A DEDICATION TO THE WORLD

** SKIP THIS SECTION AFTER THE 2ND REPEAT

* SKIP THIS SECTION AFTER THE 1ST REPEAT

THE CHILDREN RUN FOR OUR FUTURE

One-by-one the children dedicate their run to whatever they choose.

The facilitator adds spontaneous activities and suggests images.

Children choose an adult from the circle to run with.

Once everyone is running, the group will inevitably arrive at their own rhythm and groupings.

OUR CHILDREN RUN FOR

The Run

The Run Begins

Coda

JOIN US!

3RD CYCLE THE CHILDREN RUN

The outer circle - a vigorous run

The middle circle - a moderate run

The inner circle - easy steps

When a runner needs to rest they can stand in the center around the musicians.

One person at a time stands with out-stretched arms.

With conviction and strength, each person declares their dedication and begins their run until everyone is included.

The musicians establish a steady unifying pulse.

Return to Tree

Musicians lead and the group forms 2 lines facing each other.

Starting at the tail-end of the line, participants form pairs.

They acknowledge each other as they move through a bridge.

This continues until everyone passes the musicians honoring their musical contribution.

FEAST

GATHER AT THE TREE.

A FEAST AWAITS.

During the late 1980s, I was asked to apply my work in the healing arts to people with cancer and HIV infection. From this experience, I saw the fear surrounding AIDS, a disease that seemed to have no boundaries and no cure. Rampant mostly in the gay community at that time, AIDS brought up the need for work that would confront social and internalized homophobia. There was a lot of ignorance about how the disease was transmitted. Many people feared being in contact with those who had been infected. The disease held a frightening taboo, and my extended dance community was in real crisis. My collaborators and I decided to dedicate the 1989 dance to people living with HIV and AIDS.

We sent out an invitation to participants from previous *Circle the Earth* dances, students, dance colleagues, Positive Motion (a special AIDS-related group with which I was already working), and a group of people with cancer who also were working with me. We asked them to join us in a different kind of healing dance. We stated that the intention was to heal the fear, isolation, and prejudice surrounding the AIDS crisis. Over one hundred people from all walks of life came. Despite this diversity, we had one common goal: to see if, through movement and art, we could heal our community and ourselves. Could we dance to break through the prejudices and fears that separated us? Could we learn to trust the wisdom of our bodies as much as the wisdom of our minds? What followed was *Circle the Earth: Dancing with Life on the Line* (detailed in chapter 3).

Everything I had done up to that point led to this rendition of *Circle the Earth*, and this was the first time that the goal was so intimately tied to the performers. The dance for the capture of the killer, the dance for peace, the dance of caring for the environment, of trying to get things right between humanity and nature, were all crucial endeavors, but all existed at some distance from the dancers. In this case, we were dancing for the health of the people in the dance, and this lent another level of intensity to the ritual. The felt commitment to this healing became the life force of the dance. Everyone was dancing both for themselves and for one another, in both real *and* ritual time and space. This was true as well for the people who came to witness the dance, who were either HIV-positive themselves or the friends and family of people who were. Everyone had a personal reason to be in this dance, a fact that reinforced my belief that when we gather our intention about our actions as we dance, we may be able to effect change.

The impact of the community healing that came about as a result of the performance of *Circle the Earth: Dancing with Life on the Line* was so great that we continued doing this particular version of the dance through 1991. Since that time, *Circle the Earth* in its entirety has not

Anna declaring intention for Earth Run, 1990s. © Jay Graham Photographer.
Anna Halprin Papers; courtesy of Museum of Performance and Design, San Francisco.

Anna and grandson Micah Vassau in *Planetary Dance*, 1990s. Photographer unknown.
Anna Halprin Papers; courtesy of Museum of Performance and Design, San Francisco.

been danced in my local community, although it has been performed in other parts of the world. The *Planetary Dance*, however, still takes place on Mount Tamalpais each year, as well as at other locations around the world. In 2015, for example, hundreds of people participated in *Planetary Dances* in different communities across the globe, from North and South America to Europe, the Middle East, and Asia.

Circle the Earth:
Dancing with Life on the Line

3

Circle the Earth: Dancing with Life on the Line began in 1989 with a nine-day workshop and performance, and it was repeated in 1991. We chose the subtitle "Dancing with Life on the Line" because the core performers were people facing life-threatening illnesses. Many had AIDS, some had cancer, and some had chronic fatigue or other diseases. AIDS became our focus due to its clear and present danger, and because its high visibility and frightening implications made it an important metaphor for challenging life and death. But the dance was not really about AIDS, it was about healing on the physical, emotional, mental, and spiritual levels. Our intention was to bring people together to commit to a larger purpose—the grand cycle of life and death and its mysterious unfolding. By revealing our personal relationship to this central human drama, we were able to create an event that was both specific to ourselves and in dialogue with the larger life forces surrounding us. By making this ritual and confronting these social and community issues, we were working to heal our own personal fears, isolation, and prejudices.

In detailing this one specific workshop, I hope to provide a more concrete guide to the philosophy shaping any particular rendition of *Circle the Earth* as well as the development of community-based rituals in general. This chapter is a combination of manual, eyewitness report, and description of the Five Stages of Healing as they applied to our workshop and performance process. *Circle the Earth* is a series of moving ceremonies and calls to action that create a contemporary dance ritual. The final performance is comprised of a series of scores, each with its own intention, in alignment with the Five Stages of Healing.

The workshop presented here is not a model workshop, a step-by-step guide appropriate for any group. It is a selective history of a particular group's time together and admittedly not a completely accurate one. Even twenty-some years ago, when work on this book first started, my collaborators and I couldn't always remember exactly when something had occurred. We would consult numerous written accounts and interview transcripts, but sometimes they contradicted each other. Although what was experienced was clear, the day on which it happened sometimes was not. Despite these difficulties in reconstructing the precise sequence of activities and events, this book presents a day-by-day account, as I believe this will give a clear sense of the process involved. Some scores were done only in the workshop and not in the performance. These scores teach various movement and group awareness skills and provide a useful context for the enactment of the performance scores. Many different levels of preparation are necessary to bring a large group together in this kind of consensual activity. It is not enough to teach a group the performance scores presented here and expect to create a ritual. A big part of the work of the facilitators is creating a group sense, a group identity, and a group experience. Many of the exercises designed to impart movement skills also aim to cultivate this group sense. They are devoted to deepening the experience of the individual within the group, another crucial aspect in the creation of a contemporary ritual.

What really matters in creating this kind of ritual is for each individual to have the time and space to find a personal, subjective connection to the larger, collective score. Participants need to feel themselves in the movement, to infuse their own experiences into it. Although the series of scores for the *Circle the Earth* performance evolved from previous workshops, I recognize that each group is different. There is always the possibility of reshaping the dance and including new scores if enough people have similar subjective experiences that call for this—which is what happened in the workshop for *Dancing with Life on the Line*. If that ever stops— the power of individuals to reinvest and reinfuse heart and meaning into a collective myth—the dance will die. A primary role of the facilitator of the ritual is making sure that the personal and the collective myths mesh in a generative feedback loop. My hope is that in reading this account of our workshop and performance experience, the connections between myth and ritual, the healing process, and the supportive development of community will become clearer. As you will see, our original score for the performance was altered by the input of the participants of the group. This is always true when we engage in the process of collective creativity. No two groups will do the same score in the same way (unless the score is very closed). What is exciting to me, and what I hope will excite you, is how the scores resonate with people's lives and how they change to fit a community's needs.

It is important to note another aspect of the collaborative process behind *Circle the Earth*, which I strongly recommend as a method when you create your own dance rituals. Performance is a multimedia art form calling for highly interactive collaborations between artists. The successful production of a dance often includes the contributions not only of the dancers but also of graphic artists, visual artists, musicians, writers, and actors. For *Circle the Earth: Dancing with Life on the Line*, I worked with a narrator/scriptwriter, a co-leader who directed the group in movement exercises, a costume designer, a set designer, a musical director, and various musicians. Without their intelligence and support, the dance would have been much less than it was. In workshops like the one described here, a constant interaction between the dancers and the various media generates rich ideas, encourages greater personal investment, and activates a pluralistic and cooperative method of creation reflective of the philosophy of the dance itself. We are all part of a team working together to create this event. This brings us close together and stimulates our individual creativity in exciting and dynamic ways. Not only is there interaction between performers and collaborators within the work, but there is also interaction among the collaborators themselves, each taking on different roles in an easy, shifting manner. Although my focus is on leading the group, shaping the dance, and coordinating the collaborators, there are many instances in which I will give input to the other artists and they in turn will give me suggestions about the development of the scores or how to resolve a particular problem.

The musicians' contribution in particular creates a cohesive force, giving everyone the same impetus to move and drawing us together. The music also creates an order for the piece. It is important for the music to develop with the dance so that it neither moves nor directs the dancers, but supports and offers another dimension to our movement. This way of working together is a true collaboration. Make sure you find musicians who can support the strength of your dance with the strength of their sounds. Their importance to the dance cannot be underestimated.

In addition to artistic collaborators, I make use of consultants whenever I hit an impasse with scoring or become overwhelmed by the group dynamics. Such support is invaluable. My friend James Nixon made a practice of taking me on a meditative walk before any *Circle the Earth* workshop or performance—providing a time to gain the personal direction and inner guidance needed to lead others. In the workshops I use trained facilitators to lead support groups and provide individual attention so that individuals don't get lost in the group. These facilitators have usually been graduates of the Tamalpa Institute or people who are famil-

Some Thoughts on Cultural Differences

To facilitate diverse groups in community dance it is important to be sensitive to cultural differences within the group. In some cultures, for example, it may be awkward or prohibitive for men and women to engage in touch or invite direct eye contact. As my daughter Rana Halprin reminds me: "Every culture has a distinctive worldview. To authentically engage multicultural experience, it is essential to acknowledge a culture's unique embodied history and symbolic constructs. The facilitator and participants should recognize and appreciate the singular expressive modalities within ethnicity. The process of real pluralism requires a time commitment to explore and learn from the inherited artistic memory of other groups. In this manner, the opportunity to create scores that reflect and incorporate alternate origin myths greatly enriches the creative process. We enhance the notion of a universal dance by celebrating the relevance of the deep pulse of diversity."

iar with the process of active listening. Their presence ensures that each person stays connected to the larger whole and has someone to turn to express emotions when that opportunity isn't provided in the group context. Particularly important is my workshop co-leader, who not only conducts various movement warm-ups but also provides participants with a special perspective on what their needs might be from day to day, both physically and emotionally. Running a workshop of this scope is a huge task and responsibility; when you take it on for yourself, I hope you will have a trusted team of helpers by your side and at your back.

A mundane but critical dimension of this event that needs to be mentioned is its administration—all the business aspects that go into creating an event of this scale—including finances, publicity, mailings, graphic design, fund-raising, and the myriad logistical problems that inevitably arise, from rental agreements to insurance coverage. Everybody working on administration needs to be in alignment with the intentions and goals of the ritual to maintain its integrity of purpose and to communicate an accurate message about the dance to the public. No one, for instance, was turned away from this workshop or performance for lack of funds. Although advance or advocacy pieces about *Circle the Earth* were encouraged, critics were not invited to write reviews of this event, as it was not intended as that kind of performance.

What follows is a description of one dance that I hope will inspire you to create your own community rituals. Within the particularities of this experience is a more generic format that others can adapt to fit their needs. The point is to convey an *approach* to creating community dances as much as to tell the story of this particular dance. I encourage you to look at what you are doing in your community in its own light. Once you have a sense of the structure we used, make your dances responsive to your community, using all of your creative and healing resources.

DAY 1. *The Beginning of Community*

The first workshop for *Dancing with Life on the Line* begins on the day before Easter Sunday, in the last week of March 1989. All the participants meet in the gymnasium of our local high school on that first day. On the second day, Easter Sunday, we gather on Mount Tamalpais, where past participants in the dance join us. To accommodate different people's schedules, we split into two groups for the next four days, with about seventy coming in the daytime (from 10:00 to 5:00) and thirty in the evening (from 6:30 to 9:30). Both groups essentially learn the same scores, although obviously the daytime participants have more time to explore them. The two groups then come together again on the following weekend for the final three days of the workshop and the performance.

To start, we stand in a circle and count off. When we reach 100, everyone cheers, and then we continue around the circle, counting 135 people who have arrived to participate in this *Circle the Earth*. I am amazed that so many people have come together, despite their fears, despite social pressures, despite the difficulty of facing the unknown. The members of the group range from fifteen to seventy-five years old. There are people challenging AIDS or cancer, along with caregivers and friends, as well as dancers from the Tamalpa Institute and around the world. The diversity of the participants, whether trained in dance or not, is impressive, including teachers, therapists, clergy, businesspeople, students, and health professionals. Our task on this first day is to forge a sense of community, to find a common language and discover a way of dancing together. This is a day to establish basic values about ritual-making, introduce ourselves to each other, and make connections between what we do, how we feel, and what this means. As we build our community, we will learn to both appreciate our differences and find our commonalities.

On the first day, it is important to give people the opportunity to express their differences before they find their similarities. We learn about each other through movement, writing, vocalizing, drawing, and conversation. Ideas are presented in simple, nonthreatening ways to enable everyone to participate fully. On the first day of the workshop, we do scores that generate a common experience and begin to create a group sensibility. They are not performance scores; they are scores intended to build a foundation upon which the performance will rest. The performance will only be as clear and as solid as our own relationships with one another.

At the very start we try to help the dancers realize the challenges inherent in making a dance that has personal and social meaning. We let them know that before embarking on this journey, they need to understand that *Circle the Earth* is a ritual with the potential to affect their lives in profound ways. The path they have chosen is not an easy one and requires their full commitment. It is a path that must be chosen over and over again. When they feel sore or tired, sad or afraid, bored or angry, confused, dismayed or embarrassed, they need to realize that we cannot move toward healing on a global level by retreating from our own experiences. We must stick with it, go through it. We cannot change the world without changing ourselves.

I show the group a chart of the process we will be using. On it are three words—movement, emotions, and visualizations—with arrows between them. These arrows can go in any direction, indicating that sometimes you might start with an emotion and find a movement. Other times you might start a movement and discover that it connects to emotion. Or you might start with an image that then stimulates movement. It can go in any direction. The chart also shows an inner circle and an outer circle. The very personalized experience that everybody has, the one unique to that individual's life and needs, is the smaller, inner circle. Then there is the larger circle, in which we all share a similar image, movement, or emotion. It is important that both these circles are constantly interacting. If you go only for the personal, you won't be able to create something that connects to other people. It will be more of an individually therapeutic experience. If you are only in the outer circle, then the experience may seem too abstract, something that has been imposed on you. You haven't really felt it yourself first.

To help clarify the personal experience, we encourage everyone to keep a journal of his or her experience as it evolves day to day. The way an individual personally responds to the overall score, his or her images, emotions, and stories, all need to be attended to with care for they hold clues to the ongoing impact of the ritual on that person's life—an impact that will slowly grow and shape itself over the days, both in and out of the dance. We also take time at the start to reassure people about some of the confusions that may arise during the workshop and performance. One of the first confusions that many participants face concerns the structure of the dance. Some are surprised and disappointed to learn that much of the dance is already set; others are equally surprised and worried that so much is left open-ended. "How can I honestly commit to a structure I had so little part in creating?" some people ask. "How will I express my own ideas and emotions?" Others may hesitate: "I'm not a dancer or an artist. Why expect me to create my own movements, much less perform them in front of an audience, when I've never performed in my life? Can't you just teach me the steps?" Still others wonder: "Will it work to have trained artists working side by side with people who have no previous training?"

We want everyone to understand that it does work to have people with different levels of skill create together. In fact, that is the only way this particular dance can work. *Circle the Earth* is specifically designed for a large group of diverse people—people from many walks of life, backgrounds, skills, talents, and perspectives. This diversity is what gives the dance its human vitality and relevance. Healing a social issue—whether it be war, violence, racism or, in the instance of the workshop described here, AIDS—is something no one group or kind of people can do alone. We all have to do it together. Although a new dance could be made from scratch each time a new group performs, that would require a lot more time—much more than a week. It is not possible for such a large group of people to take time off from work, family, and other commitments to spend the many weeks, months, even years necessary to create a new dance. It is wonderful that so many people can commit to nine days, and amazing that powerful and moving performances can be created within this time. It's a miracle what people can create when they are highly motivated and working cooperatively. Having a common intention, strong motivation, and a process of collective creativity—the RSVP Cycles—all contribute to allowing this to happen.

On this first day, to set a tone of sharing and communality, we begin with a food ceremony. Butcher paper has been laid out as a "tablecloth" in the space, with bread at the center. The bread is blessed and passed around so everyone can share the same loaves. A participating vocalist sings a welcoming song and people introduce themselves: the scriptwriter, musicians, facilitators, workshop assistants, people who have danced *Circle the Earth* before, people new to the dance, people from other countries, the youngest and the oldest, people from Positive Motion (men challenging AIDS), Women with Wings (women challenging AIDS), and the Moving Towards Life group (people challenging cancer). There are also special caregivers, participants invited by those with life-threatening illnesses to offer support and a sense of safety when emotional issues arise. As different people are introduced, we begin to get a sense of ourselves. The mood is one of apprehension, animation, and anticipation.

I am excited and challenged when everyone gathers. I have such high hopes: I want this dance to reveal the joys, sorrows, grief, and fears of the participants—and to reveal the ways we grapple with prejudice, isolation, and death. Hopefully, through the process of creating this dance, all of us will find the support, strength, and power to overcome our daily anxieties around AIDS and cancer and, through the performance, we will be able to share what we learn with our families, lovers, and friends. I want this dance to be a community healing experience and the workshop to be a safe place for all of us to express what is deep in our hearts. I wish to participate in a true search for a living myth and ritual that will bring us together in the act of celebrating life. We are embarking on a hero's journey and as the first day of the workshop begins, I realize this will be the most difficult task of my career. It will take all the knowledge accumulated during my personal and professional life to meet the challenge. I am grateful to have such wonderful collaborators—friends and colleagues who have been with me for many years, sharing the same hopes and desires. I know I can't achieve my hopes without their insights and contributions. I enter the workshop with a series of scores—some carefully thought-out plans—but no fixed outcome.

There are so many souls to track in this large group. With this many participants, it is important to provide help, clarification, encouragement, provocation, comfort, and a place to be heard in smaller, more intimate environments. For this reason, support groups of about ten people each are organized after lunch. Each group has a facilitator. These groups meet each day during the workshop and become a place to share experiences and resolve difficulties. These smaller groups play an important role in creating an environment of democratic sharing. They allow people who do not feel comfortable sharing in a larger group to be heard. They make it clear that everyone's voice is welcome and needed to create this dance. From a logistical and organizational perspective, it is not time-efficient to try to have discussions with very large groups of people and to track and utilize everything that is being expressed. The support groups honor our intention to integrate each person's experience into the experience of the whole group. The facilitators assist in this goal and provide a strong support system during the workshop, without which the larger group could not accomplish so much in such a short time. Planned activities in the support groups are used to promote a positive, high-spirited yet protective atmosphere. At the end of each day, facilitators give me, as the leader, a summary of the feedback from their support groups. I then incorporate the groups' responses into the overall scheme of the dance, ensuring that individual voices are heard and contribute to the development of the dance.

My main collaborators have all been associated with me for a long time, and the facilitators in this group have all performed *Circle the Earth* before or participated in a specific weeklong training in communication and scoring skills to prepare for this role. All of these collaborating facilitators share a similar philosophy and understanding of dance, and every one of the facilitators has a grounding in the Life/Art Process.[9] When setting up your support team for a community dance ritual, take care to work with collaborators who share your views, who extend your own personal skill set, and who are flexible enough to play a variety of support roles throughout the process.

THE NAME GAME

Once the support groups have been established, we play the Name Game. I was introduced to the idea of the Name Game in a group session with Fritz Perls, the Gestalt psychologist. When he used this process, he wanted the group to learn how to concentrate and pay attention to each other. I further developed this score, bringing in the elements of movement, teamwork, and performance skills. The intention for doing the Name Game at the beginning of a workshop is to foster the sense of a comfortable and friendly environment, as well as to encourage spontaneity. Laughter and play help people relax and diminish their inhibitions in group situations. In this dance, people have an opportunity to create together, to perform and to witness, and to laugh and cry with one another.

Intention:	Learn each other's names.
	Get to know each other through movement and sound.
	Learn a collective way to create together.
SCORE	
Time:	Approximately 1 hour, depending on how many people are in the group.[10]
Space:	Clusters of circles spread evenly throughout the room.
People:	Groups of 7–10 in a circle. (Groups are same as support groups.)

Activities: The leader gives step-by-step directions to facilitate this score and remains conscious of the time needed for participants to finish each part of the score.

Part I

1. Sit in a circle, breathe, and look around.
2. First person: begin by saying your first name together with an arm gesture. Person to the right: repeat the first person's name and gesture, followed by your own name and your own gesture. Keep repeating this around the circle until everyone has added his or her name and gesture.
3. Stand and repeat step 2, expanding the arm gesture into whole body movements.
4. Now replace names with sounds, going around the circle, repeating each participant's sound and gesture. Try to enlarge the movements and to use your entire body.
5. Everyone in the group: perform the whole sequence of movements and sounds in unison.
6. Explore new combinations using a greater range of space, moving into and out of the center of the circle.
7. Take a moment to look around the circle at each person. Do you know everybody's name?
8. Take approximately a minute per person to share your experience of performing and working together.

Part II

1. Join with three or four other groups.
2. Each group: perform the score for the others. When not performing, witness the other performances.

This dance is done in a humorous and playful way. Each group's performance is uniquely different, as are the individuals within each group. The movements may be performed in a variety of ways—from spontaneous to carefully planned. The witnessing groups show an enthusiastic appreciation for each performance and a sense of bonding begins.

The Name Game introduces, in a nonthreatening way, the idea that dances are based on real situations and that we can effectively respond to real-life needs through movement. When the workshop begins, participants may feel uneasy in a new situation, and they may not know everybody's name. This score provides a friendly, welcoming environment and a fun way to learn new names through dancing, speaking, performing, and witnessing.

TRAILS

Like the Name Game, the next score—Trails—focuses on differences, allowing people to be valued for their individuality and at the same time practice working together as a group. The Name Game is nonconfrontational and inclusive. Everyone's movements are witnessed and experienced by everyone else. It is about the simple sharing of names. Trails is the first score that invites direct physical contact among participants. It combines opportunities for both risky and safe behavior. It is risky because participants use touch to complete the score; to keep it safe the group must use touch in a way that is not threatening or invasive. The score is enacted in a slow and careful manner, with eyes blindfolded, which creates a nonpersonal, kinesthetic experience.

The Name Game demands that you look and pay attention to what is happening outside you; Trails demands that you look inside and pay attention to that landscape. Because participants are blindfolded, they need to rely on their kinesthetic sense to guide their movements. Being blindfolded requires a certain level of trust, yet it also gives permission to touch others without knowing precisely who or what you are touching. This aids people in overcoming any conditioned experience of touch as necessarily a sexual contact. All the senses except sight, which tends to be overused, are employed in this exercise. Hands also tend to overwork, so people are encouraged to use their backs, legs, feet, face, shoulders, and hips to feel their way along the path.

One note about Trails—some participants may hesitate to engage in this activity because they have a history of trauma or unwanted touching, or there may be cultural differences that make touching problematic. It is important to be aware of this possibility and not to force anyone to do this exercise if they feel uncomfortable. Instructing participants not to reach with their hands but instead to make gentle contact with other parts of their bodies can reduce the likelihood that anyone will feel touched in a way that is uncomfortable for them.

Intention: Build trust and intimacy.

SCORE

Time: 30 minutes.

Space: Throughout the room in lines.

People: All participants, working in support groups.

Activities:

1. Blindfold one person.

2. Form a linear path away from the blindfolded person with the rest of the group, using all levels (standing, bending, kneeling, sitting, lying) and staying in physical contact with the person in front of and behind you.

3. Once this "trail" is in place, if you are the blindfolded person, follow it to the end by moving slowly from one body to another along the line.

4. Remove the blindfold and look at the path you've traveled.

5. Share your one strongest image and emotion with your group.

6. Put the blindfold on another member of the group, form a new trail, and repeat the score until everyone has performed it.

Again, in performing this score, many people need to be reminded that they can find their way along the trail using parts of the body other than the hands. They are encouraged to explore. Touching other people with eyes closed gives rise to an array of responses: humor, timidity, fear, excitement, confusion, and tenderness. One participant says, "I got totally lost in space. I went backwards and forwards—couldn't find the end." Another imagines himself as a hunted animal, embodying a wary silence.

Some groups develop challenging trails that require climbing up on bodies; others are so complex the blindfolded person gets lost. The succession of trails developed by each group demonstrates a variety of ways in which individual contributions build a collective form. The people forming the trail start taking more risks, climbing on one another's bodies to create paths that lead vertically as well as horizontally. The facilitators must take care that it doesn't become too risky.

THE VORTEX DANCE

The first two scores involve individual differences. The next score is the first in which we try to find consensus. The group is ready now to explore this possibility because we have had time to express our individuality in the earlier scores. In this score, called the Vortex Dance, we rely on all our senses, with a strong emphasis on the auditory. This score allows people to find community through an open, nonverbal exchange. It is too early in the process of building community to present a totally closed score. We are still gathering resources and information about who we are as a group. Agreement in the form of structured movement cannot be imposed upon a group at this point because it might censor or inhibit people's true responses to the score. Instead, the group is guided toward consensus in a concrete way, through movement.

Intention: Build community.

SCORE

Time: 1 hour.

Space: Entire space.

People: All participants.

Activities:

1. Find your heartbeat pulsing in your wrist or neck and walk alone through the space to its pulse. Use your peripheral vision.
2. Listen to the sound of everyone's feet on the floor. Compare your walk with that of others around you, trying to find a common pulse.
3. Once everyone is walking to the same beat, the drummer will join in, reinforcing the common pulse.
4. Develop your own movement in response to the beat of the drum and to the other dancers.
5. Interact with the drum and each other, joining together in twos, threes, whatever. Allow the inspiration of the music and the other dancers to move you through space, into and out of interactions with other people. Use your voice. Breathe.
6. Find a group closure.

Finding a common beat can take more than twenty minutes or as little as five minutes. I have noticed how this task is influenced by one's cultural background. For example, when I worked with a Japanese group, it took them only a few seconds to find a common beat. In contrast, I noticed with a group in Berlin, Germany, that people drifted off to the side of the space and resisted participation as we got closer and closer to a common beat. From our later valuaction, I learned the score brought up a fear of fascism; for them, the score represented conformity, militarism, and the blind following of authority. In the United States, on the other hand, it often takes a very long time for a group to find a common pulse. Americans' quest for independence may lead to a struggle to suspend individuality.

Whatever the cultural distinctions, a pulse eventually establishes a kind of commonality that everybody can accept or agree upon. I think this is because it is reflective of something we all share—the continual beating of our hearts—which usually happens below our conscious sensing, but which guides and forms the structure and shape of our bodies and our lives. Once we surrender to the group pulse, it forms a scaffold supporting complex and diverse human patterns. The alternative would be utter chaos, which has its own form, but which creates quite a different experience for individuals and for groups. If everybody just did whatever she or he wanted and recognized nothing in common, it would be very difficult to connect.

The Vortex Dance requires connecting your own heartbeat to that of others. If you are very out of step with others, it means adapting your speed as a gesture of cooperation with the group—joining into the dynamic rush of a faster pace around you or slowing down to appreciate the calmness of another pace. There is a peak moment of relief and release in the effort to find unity through consensus. Once a nonverbal consensus is established, the musicians reinforce the group by playing back its pulse with the drum. It can be a struggle for participants to give up individual will. Or it may be a relief to find yourself walking in tandem with others. You may connect with your longing for unity or your fear of surrender. It is important to let people have their own experiences of this: some people will learn that they tend to give over easily to the group; others will discover that this is uncomfortable for them or unacceptable. All of this information is useful for the dancer and for the creation of the dance, so it is important to allow people the time and space to recognize their own patterns and inclinations.

This score is the first time that the group uses the entire space as one body. And it is the first score where everyone is working together, rather than in smaller groups. Over one hundred people moving together in a huge space is exciting and powerful. I trust the chaos that initially emerges as a natural outcome with its own inherent form, and I trust that it will lead to unison action in its own way and in its own time. We will do this score over and over again throughout the course of the workshop process, each time cultivating a greater range of movement skills useful in our interactions with one another. The repetition of the score adds dimension to our social body and becomes a powerful learning opportunity, as people feel the experience of unity challenges and nourishes them.

The sense of a self-discovered collective body generates a liberating power that leads to dances of unpredictable invention, spontaneity, delight, and support. These can be seen as metaphors for a set of creative values that establish the quality and nature of the community we are becoming. Participants often find a partner first and gradually move in small groups. Small groups become bigger groups forming counterpoint rhythms and contrasting formations, bouncing off one another in astonishingly complex and inventive ways. No choreographer could possibly design the endless rhythms and patterns that emerge. The group may come together first in wild, ecstatic movements; jump up as if to explore

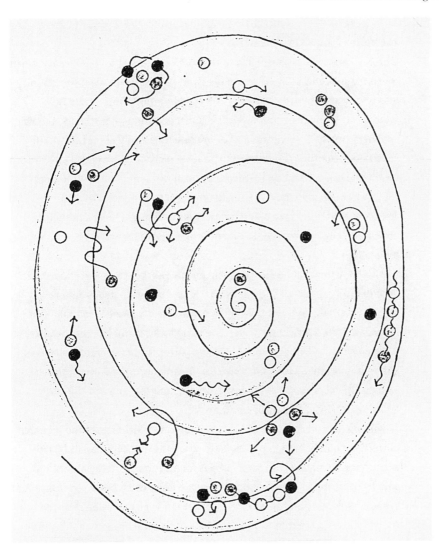

the outer vertical spaces; then finally sink to the ground like one body. Voices often swell to reach a peak, then phase out in a gentler hum.

Capable of inspiring patterns of chaos as well as patterns of geometric cohesion, the Vortex score is very permissive and open-ended. Throughout the dance, participants make choices. They choose their partners; they choose how they're going to move with those partners; they choose when to expand from partnerships to family clusters; they choose which movements to do in those clusters. They choose leaders and followers; they choose when to blend. By the time they come together as a single voice, the dance is an unspoken but freely chosen consensus.

This is the most open score in the whole process. Open scores require a great degree of imagination, creativity, and spontaneity, and this score requires that everyone use all their movement resources to come

The Vortex Dance as a Natural Pattern

One day I was riding a horse in a redwood forest in Northern California, when my horse suddenly stopped at the river's edge. I looked to see if something was wrong and then saw a school of fish swimming in formation. They were small, silvery fish, and when the sun shone through the water, I could see them clearly. They swam in one direction for a few feet and, in a flash, switched to another direction. With another flick of their fins and tails, they swam and turned back on themselves and, moving in a curve, alternated their smooth gliding movement with an abrupt change of direction. They repeated this dance many times. Then, as unexpectedly as they had appeared, they swam away. I could no longer see them and my horse moved on.

Lauren Artress, an honorary canon of Grace Cathedral in San Francisco, describes an experience she had with a school of fish that was almost identical to mine, only she goes on to say that Native Americans call what I witnessed the *dance of the fishes*. She says, "I had stumbled onto a dance, a sacred ritual, a divine secret of invisible patterns throughout all of nature, patterns imprinted within each species. The migration patterns of the whales, the hibernation of the bears, and the mating dance of the birds, are all woven into the web of creation."[11]

Among my favorite examples of these invisible patterns are the monarch butterflies that fly back to particular trees on the northern coast of California each spring to mate. They travel from as far away as the Rocky Mountains and, by some miraculous instinct, know precisely which tree to approach. What is even more amazing is the fact that it is the generation once removed from the experience that has this instinct encoded in its biology. Even though these creatures have never been to this tree before or taken this journey, they know where to go.

together in consensus. Dances like this address a far-reaching question: Can everyone dance? My many years of experience tell me the answer is a most emphatic "Yes!"

I am fascinated by similar dances found in nature (see above). I believe that we as human beings, like the fish and the butterflies I observed, have encoded, instinctual patterns in our cellular awareness, and I have seen groups of people discover them while dancing. I've been told that if you put two living cells in separate petri dishes, their beat and pulse will remain unrelated and differentiated. But if you put those same two cells in the same dish, within seconds their beats will begin pulsing in unison.

The same thing happens when people are working together. Such a group may start out in a seemingly random state, but this apparent randomness will soon find its own ordering system. When enough people move together with a common purpose, an amazing force, an ecstatic rhythm, eventually takes over. People stop moving as individuals and begin to move as if they were parts of a single body, not in uniform motion, but in deeply interrelated ways. In these fundamental movements, people seem to be tracing out the forms and patterns of a larger organism, communicating as one being moved by a group mind and spirit.

FIRST SELF-PORTRAIT DRAWING: WHO AM I?

After the experience of group unity with the Vortex score, we return to the self and draw the first in a series of self-portraits. Drawing a self-portrait has many functions. It provides a shift of focus from a physically active stance to one of rest and stillness. It defines in an objective, visible form the participant's subjective state of being. It brings the group experience back to the self and begins the process of discovering the individual's unique story, his or her personal myth, which is further developed during the workshop. It confirms the experience of individuality within the group. Again and again, I see how no two people ever draw the same self-portrait. There are no two people alike in the gym where we hold the workshop, or in the country, or in the world. The self-portrait drawings further establish our practice of including each person's individuality within the experience of our commonalities. This score establishes an awareness of various dimensions of our experience: physical, emotional, and mental or imaginal. Drawing and sharing the self-portraits create opportunities to appreciate the diversity within the group because each portrait is so different. Another self-portrait will be done at the end of the workshop to appreciate and integrate our rite of passage and the changes we have experienced.

Intention:	Externalize an image of yourself.
	Assimilate the experiences of the day.
SCORE	
Time:	1 hour (may vary as needed).
Space:	Individually scattered in the room.
People:	All participants.

Activities:

1. Using oil pastels and a large piece of paper (18 × 24 inches), draw a picture of how you see yourself right now.
2. When you have finished, select three words to describe the picture:

a "physical" word for what you see objectively, an "emotional" word for the feeling evoked by the picture, and an "image" word for what you associate with the picture.

3. Create a sentence: "I am …" followed by your three words.
4. Go to your support group and one by one share your drawings by holding them up and saying your sentence.
5. Divide into pairs and dance your self-portrait for your partner. Place your drawing in front of you, letting it become the inspiration for your movement. Dance it three times, each time emphasizing a different word in your sentence.
6. Partners: witness the dance and, when the dancer is done, respond with your own experience of the dance, from the three levels of awareness: I saw _____ (physical); I felt _____ (emotional); and I imagined _____ (associative). Facilitators: rove from partnership to partnership to help witnesses respond nonjudgmentally.
7. Switch roles and repeat steps 5 and 6.
8. After everyone has had a chance to dance his or her self-portrait, hang the drawings on the wall and go around the room, looking at each person's drawing.
9. Go back to your support group and share your observations, emotions, and thoughts about the experience.

This first portrait is a starting point and provides a way for participants to see the transformations created by dancing. Some people draw representational pictures of themselves; others create more abstract and emotional images; still others fill their drawings with symbols. "I did a very peaceful, shining self-portrait," one participant says. "My words were: round and pulsing, the moon, excited." Everyone is fascinated when they go around the room and look at one another's drawings. The uniqueness of each drawing and each person is evident. The opportunity for each participant to delve deeply into her or his personal mythology and share it with another can be very fulfilling, another opportunity for self-awareness and deeper community relationships.

A SPECIAL CEREMONY: PRESENTATION OF THE FEATHERS

The first day of the workshop is an orientation to each other and to a way of creating together. At the end of the day, we orient the group to the activities of the next day. On our second day, we will be meeting outdoors on Mount Tamalpais, rain or shine, to participate in a community enactment of the *Planetary Dance*, a dance for peace among peoples and peace with the earth (see chapters 2 and 4). As this takes place outside, on the mountain, the second day of the workshop serves as an orientation to the natural world; the Presentation of the Feathers is symbolic of the transition to this world.

The Presentation of the Feathers is a ceremonial score particular to this workshop and not exactly transferable to other situations. But the principle of introducing ceremony early on in the workshop process is valuable. I have discovered that this kind of ceremonial preparation, whether it takes place before our time on the mountain or before the performance itself, is necessary in the creation of ritual space. Some of what happens in this ceremony can be most simply defined as the "creation of context." During this time, we speak about the work we are doing in relationship to a lineage of related dances, the philosophy of the dance we are doing, and our hopes for it. Participants are given the history and background of the *Planetary Dance*, which they will participate in the next day, so that they can know, in effect, the actual realm they will traverse.

Certain behaviors are appropriate in ritual space, just as certain behaviors are appropriate in a temple, a bank, or your home. We impart what we know about the most respectful and positive ways to exist in ritual space. These include silence and stillness, when required, and a general respect for the order of events, whether or not all participants explicitly understand them. Sometimes in a ritual something happens that has not been explained, but it happens for a reason that has to do with the efficacy of the ritual. Within the context of ritual space, an attitude of surrender, rather than one of challenge or constant questioning, is useful. A meditative quality is not only encouraged, but also modeled at this time, laying the ground for a particular way of being in ritual space. People are asked to reflect on what the following day might mean to them. The group speaks about sharing special time with family and friends, prayer, gratitude, hope, and desire.

The ceremony is simple. As part of the next day's *Planetary Dance*, four people will carry feathers as they run up the mountain, each approaching from one of the four directions (north, south, east, west). In the workshop ceremony, we share the story of the feathers with the group, and the four runners formally receive the feathers, along with a reminder of the dedication of their run. One of the feathers we use is named Goldy, after a young golden eagle found many years ago by a park ranger. Misidentified initially as a bald eagle, she was fed a diet of vegetables instead of the red meat more suitable for a golden eagle. This improper diet permanently weakened her flight muscles so, for her own safety, she was placed in the Marin Wildlife Center rather than being released into the wild. A young woman gave me one of Goldy's feathers in 1980, and I carried that feather with me on the trails of Mount Tamalpais in one of our early dances there. In that first dance, the feather was more witness than participant, but as time passed and the ritual grew, the role of the feather grew too. By the time of the workshop for *Dancing with Life on the Line*, different people had run with Goldy all over the trails of Mount Tamalpais and even carried her to the top of Mount Whitney, the tallest peak in the lower forty-eight states. Goldy had been blessed by several spiritual leaders, including Don Jose Mitsuwa, who honored her by placing a feather from the Himalayas atop Mount Tamalpais, and Lorin Smith, who took her into the Pomo roundhouse to increase her power. She also had traveled to Switzerland, Germany, and Australia, among other places, for performances of *Circle the Earth*.

When we do the actual performance, Goldy will be run from the mountain to the performance space. The feather will circle the room, be presented to the witnesses, and then set in a place of honor to become part of the dance. At the end of the ritual, Goldy will leave the dance as the performers circle out from the center with the image of birds sending a message of peace and healing out into the world. Like all ceremonial objects, Goldy is both a tool and a vessel, a giver and a receiver. She is an expression of our power to transform, acting as a link between worlds. As she enters the room, she links the outside world with the inside world of the performance. As she is taken out, she retraces that path, carrying the story of what happened in the dance. She is both a material object (a feather) and a symbol for flight, a transcendence of the earthbound aspects of human life. In this way she connects earth and sky, the material and the spiritual vision. Having traveled from the "useless" context of a weakened bird's wing to the "useful" context of *Circle the Earth*, Goldy connects the images of despair and hope, exemplifying the possibility of transformation in the most troubling circumstances.

For me, there is a very personal connection to the story of Goldy. One year, as I told the story of Goldy at the *Planetary Dance*, four large black birds arrived, circled overhead while the story was being told, and then flew off. When this happened again the next year, I was filled with awe. A friend asked me to tell my personal story about a bird. At first I didn't want to speak because the story seemed too private, but then I thought that perhaps if I opened my heart, others would too. When I had cancer, I left the hospital weak, vulnerable, and confused about my life. Why had this happened to me? What did I do wrong? Was I being punished? Could

I survive the ordeal and endure the pain? Would this be something I'd live with for the rest of my life? Would I be able to dance again? I was not sure if I would live or die, and I was so drained that I didn't know if I cared.

As I lay in bed, I dreamed that a black bird flew into my room and sat on the blanket. I was afraid. I tried to shout, but no sound came out. I tried to run but my legs wouldn't move. In Jewish tradition, the black bird symbolizes the angel of death who comes to take the dying home to Zion. I was sure that this bird was my angel of death, come to take me away. Suddenly my doubts left me. I knew I didn't want to leave. I wanted to go on with my life.

The bird began to talk to me in its own language. Gradually, I relaxed. There was nothing else in my consciousness except that black bird sitting by my side. I even touched its smooth and silky feathers. It trembled slightly and its thin pink legs pranced delicately. Coming from its throat was a soft, guttural vibrating sound. After we got to know each other, the bird said I could stay but only if I made a firm vow to continue to dance, and that my dances would be for the people—for love and for life. I reached out and stroked the bird, as if to say, "Yes, I promise." The bird hopped around in a circle three times and said, "I will circle around you from time to time and watch over you." Then it flew away.

On the mountain, when the black birds circled overhead during the *Planetary Dance*, I felt a sense of wonder. The birds flew away in formation, swooping, circling, gliding, darting. We silently watched them disappear over the hill. I imagined that they were messengers, taking our story to the others who were dancing with us all around the world, after watching over me like guardian angels.

UNIFYING DANCE FOR CLOSURE

At the end of the first day, we do a summation score for the group, just as we did a summation score for the individual in the form of the Self-Portrait. The "Snake" Dance[12] is designed for the group to maintain contact while moving around and seeing one another, touching each other, and dancing in rhythm together.

Intention:	Unify the group.
	See the individual in the context of the whole.
SCORE	
Time:	30 minutes (or more, depending on size of group).
Space:	Entire space.
People:	All participants.

Bringing the Group Together / Designing for Diversity of Expression

Here are questions to consider as you start your community dance ritual:

What issue brings your group together?

Do you have trusted collaborators, advisors, and consultants working with you?

How might you introduce the participants to each other and put them at ease?

What scores might help your participants laugh and move together freely?

What scores might help your group begin to bond?

Do your scores help participants address the questions: Where am I? Who am I with? What are we doing?

What kind of support groups might provide for everyone's safety and encourage full expression?

Activities:

1. Everybody join in a big circle. Hold hands loosely, without gripping, so that you can easily let go.

2. Drummer (or other musician): start a steady beat.

3. Break the circle at one point, forming a curving line with a head and a tail. "Head" person: begin walking, leading the line in a weaving pattern, folding in and out without breaking the line. Keep it simple.

4. Everybody move to the same pulse, although you can vary your foot patterns. Make visual contact with everyone you pass, but avoid talking.

5. As the movement ripples down the line, it can acquire a lot of energy. If you feel that the line is moving too fast or pulling you, let go of the hand of the person in front and initiate a new weaving line. Remain open to letting go of one line and joining another, always moving to the pulse.

6. Eventually find a way to bring the spiraling to a close in the center. (Sometimes outside instruction may be needed to facilitate this.)

7. Improvise with singing and chanting.

In this dance, the line of dancers forms a shape that keeps folding back on itself. As the dancers move in this formation, the path created enables everyone in the circle to see everyone else and to make visual contact. As the flow and pace of the dance quickens, the energy generated through the participants' connections to one another expands. The dance facilitates the coming together of a community as each dancer witnesses every other member of the circle and is in turn witnessed in the act of dancing. This score usually ends in a close cluster in the center of the space.

DAY 2. Planetary Dance

On the first day, the work of the group members is to orient themselves to one another. On the second day, when the group goes to the mountain to participate in the *Planetary Dance* (described in chapter 4), it is beginning to orient itself to the world, to the larger circle of life. Our dance, which is open to everyone, is dedicated to our brothers and sisters with AIDS. We are there to discover our place in the pattern, to find our spiritual identities, to both give strength to the mountain and gain strength from her for the task before us. By going up and down the mountain and honoring north, east, south, and west, we trace the six cardinal directions that are the warp and woof of our lives, the web on which we are woven. It is important that we are doing the *Planetary Dance* outdoors, because it's through our relationship to the sun above us and the earth under our feet that we come to know where we are in the pattern of life. Remembering where we are is essential for remembering who we are.

People make their own paths to the mountain—running, walking, or riding up to our gathering site, alone or with others. The intention is to make the journey creative and meaningful. As one participant describes, "I have always hesitated to commit myself to long hikes, from fear of humiliation if I couldn't finish. I really felt so great that I made the commitment and then *did* it. It felt like the beginning of the theme of the week: to dare something beyond what I've done and do it—just do it."

At noon everyone gathers at our chosen site to welcome the arrival of the feather runners, who have each started from a different place at the base of the mountain. Each runner tells us about his or her experience running up the mountain, generating a deep sense of commitment in all of us. One woman reports that she lost the feather along the way, was devastated, and turned around to run back down to get another feather. Running back, she found her feather on the trail. For me, this is a symbol of the risks and dangers we will face and overcome.

THE FOUR DIRECTIONS

After hearing the runners' stories, we mark the four directions of the space (for more on this process, see "Preparing the Space" in chapter 4). In this particular *Planetary Dance*, Jasper Redrobe Vassau, a member of the Cheyenne tribe, leads the marking of the four directions. Following the feather runners in a circular path, he outlines a circle on the ground with cornmeal. As everyone forms a large circle, Jasper beats a drum and leads the group in a circular dance, stepping lightly and bending low to the earth, moving counterclockwise. As he reaches the spot marking each direction, he calls out its name (northern, southern, eastern, or western) and makes a small circle inside the larger circle, sprinkling cornmeal on the ground to mark the boundaries. When all four circles are marked, the group stops and Jasper describes the symbolism of the directions in a way that resonates with our focus on a life-threatening illness.

> The eastern direction is where the sun rises, where light comes from, helping us rise.
> The southern direction is where renewed life and growth come from, giving us warmth and energy.
> The northern direction is where cold winter storms come from, where death comes from.
> The western direction is where the sun sets, where life goes, where the earth cycle reclaims and returns to spirit.

Each participant is now asked to sit in the direction "circle" that speaks most cogently to his or her experience, drawing on the symbolic interpretation just offered. We want to involve everyone in the symbolic systems we use in the creation of the dance. As we create our dance, we look to the four directions as the context of our prayers, just as we look for an inner spirit to guide us as we prepare our dance. Choosing a particular direction in which to sit is an opportunity for each participant to personalize and internalize the collective intention. Each participant then writes or draws something about her or his connection with the chosen direction. After this, people share their images and words with others in their circle.

Personalizing each direction in this way concretizes a conceptual idea. In my group (north), people draw and write about a person in their lives who has died and use this moment to grieve that loss. My close collaborator Allan Stinson reports: "I sat in a circle of the north, where death comes from. A phrase had been coming to me over and over for weeks: I am well on my way to death. So I played out loud with the words: I am

---

Planetary Dance

If a *Planetary Dance* seems appropriate for your community, consider these questions:

> Is there a specific theme, beyond the general theme of peace, that will serve your community?
>
> Who are your musicians? Can they fulfill the crucial role of maintaining the heartbeat of the dance?
>
> How might the marking of the four directions resonate for your community?
>
> What kind of closure will best serve your community?
>
> (See also chapter 4 and appendix B.)

---

well. I am well on my way. I am well on my way to death. I am well. I am well on the way. I am well on the way to death. I'm not afraid of death. But I am afraid of dying. I am well on my way to death." There are tears—and comfort is offered. Other groups are more exuberant and playful. It does not seem to matter that contrasting modes and emotions arise.

THE EARTH RUN

After creating our circle and choosing our directions, we do the Earth Run, first voicing our intention—who or what we are dancing for—and then running to a steady drumbeat in a series of concentric circles (see "The Earth Run Score" in chapter 4). The Earth Run requires cooperation. It requires group listening to the pulse and group running to that pulse. It requires maintaining a circle by moving in step with the people in front of you and behind you, being alert and not cutting in front of other runners. The structure of the dance itself reminds us of our oneness, our unity, our collective spirit. The dance simply cannot be done without generating this sense of connection in the performers.

On this Easter Sunday, we dance on a knoll high up on the mountain with fog surrounding us like a mysterious shroud. The runners call out the names of their loved ones, or a group of people, or an endangered plant or animal. After the run, there is time for people to speak of what is in their hearts. They gather in small groups and share ideas about how they might apply their personal experiences during the run and create compassionate actions in their relationships, their families, their communities, or the world. We seek to turn this dance into an opportunity for service. People who have come in previous years report about their successes in honoring their previous commitments. Gradually people break out of their groups and go alone or in small groups to their own special places on the mountain to reflect and wait for the sunset. This closes our day on the mountain.

Day 3. *Identifying the Central Theme: Life and Death*

The day after the *Planetary Dance*, we return to the school gym and start working more intensely with our theme. Each day we begin with a warm-up score, tuning up our physical bodies and sharpening our kinesthetic awareness, combined with elements from the Vortex Dance, as a way of acknowledging our community. By performing and recycling the Vortex Dance each day, we are building resources of common experience, enriching and nourishing our relationships through movement. The particular activities may vary from day to day, but the principle of an alternating rhythm of returning to the self and reaching out to many remains the same. We repeat this dance every day because it takes time to develop a language rich enough to feel comfortable with the kind of freedom and openness the Vortex Dance allows.

TUNING UP AND VORTEX VARIATIONS

Intention: Connect participants with a wide range of movement vocabulary.

SCORE

Time: 25 minutes.

Space: Entire space.

People: All participants.

Activities:

1. Bounce, shake, or do other vigorous movements to music with a strong pulse. As you do this, connect with your breath and let your breath flow through your whole body.
2. Keeping the pulse, move throughout the space, using the spaces in between people.
3. Explore your movement vocabulary. Experiment with different movement qualities, shapes, forces, and dynamics.
4. Dance alone or with others, but pay attention to the common pulse.
5. Continue exploring, beginning to interact more with others and eventually coming to a group closure.

Body-tuning scores like this one are opportunities for individuals to connect with themselves and with others. Encourage participants to maintain fidelity to their movement expression, whether or not it brings them into contact with other dancers. With body tuning, we are trying to build participants' capacity to listen to themselves as well as to the other dancers in their environment.

RISING AND FALLING

The special theme for today is rising and falling, presented as a metaphor for life and death. Rising and falling movements are selected because they are characteristic of the experiences of living and dying. It is important to select movements that are, by their very nature, essential to the theme of the dance, that evoke an experience of the theme through sensation and association. The principal characteristic of a falling movement is yielding to gravity; a rising movement goes against gravity. Uncurling the spine from a flexed, curved position to an extended position can give rise to strong associations with birth and life; falling can evoke death. Rising again from a fallen position can generate the sense of hope that comes from the rebounding, recycling energy of life. Participants are asked to explore these movements using variations in dynamics to generate individual responses and get in touch with their personal emotions about life and death.

Giving up, letting go, or falling can be characteristics of dying. Rising involves overcoming inertia and can be an affirmation of life. Participants should practice these movements in one place without moving around the room; this creates a sense of being alone within the group. In this exercise, the performer isn't asked to pretend or reenact, but to feel the experience of living or dying in that moment, to "practice" living and dying. No one is encouraged to find a pattern for going down and coming up. We do not rehearse a set of "dance" movements. We discover what is true for us in the moment. The exercise is done over and over again, not to repeat the same pattern, but to get acquainted with previously unrealized movement possibilities.

The kind of dance I am striving for is based on what is personally meaningful for the performer. Only nonstylized and ordinary movement will serve this end. Since the themes of life and death are central to *Dancing with Life on the Line*, it is important to design an open score that allows free expression of this essential human experience. We need a score that does not dictate how we should feel, but instead encourages expression of the emotions that are present for each participant. When the focus of *Circle the Earth* is on people who are living with life-threatening ill-

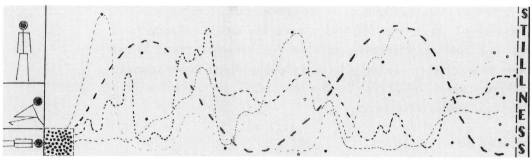

Rising and Falling score.

ness, the symbolism of the Rising and Falling score is immediate, close to home. In addition, introducing this theme defies a cultural avoidance of death and the taboo of experiencing our emotions around it. The Rising and Falling score requires a commitment from all of us, dancing alone and in a group, to perceive our stance in regard to the paradoxical nature of life and death, and to make our own offering to this truth.

Intention: Explore rising and falling as a way of evoking a personal response to the theme of life and death.

Learn how to witness and give nonjudgmental feedback.

SCORE

Time: 2 hours.

Space: Entire space.

People: All participants.

Activities:

1. As in the tune-up, start with vigorous movement to music with a strong pulse. Move throughout the space, using the spaces in between people.

2. At the facilitator's signal, stop moving and stand still. On the next drumbeat, fall to the ground in unison.

3. Begin to rise and fall in place in your own way and in your own time. Experiment with different speeds and dynamics.

4. Divide into two equal groups. First group: perform rising and falling, exploring different movement possibilities. Second group: witness their performance.

5. Witnesses: give feedback to performers without praise or criticism. What did you notice? Did they follow the score? Use "I" statements, speaking in terms of your own perceptions. For example, "When you did this, I imagined, or I felt ..."

6. Switch roles and repeat steps 4 and 5.

Performing the Rising and Falling score. Photographer unknown.

In general, the performances of this score seem to fall into two modes: kinesthetic or imagistic. Some people concentrate their awareness on the physical task of rising and falling. Others emphasize the images, associations, and emotional responses this theme evokes for them. One participant says: "I loved the sensation of the movement. I loved the reflection of myself and other people's movements in that dance and its reflections of themes in the universe. When we split into two groups and watched, I saw each rising as an inhale and each falling as an exhale, as if each rising was birth and each fall was death. It was very cyclical. I saw some people like plants, growing and budding and returning to earth. Other people were animals. One of the most profound things I saw was someone looking as though they were an entire galaxy, spinning into emptiness and ending. Everything is a cycle reflected over and over again in rising and falling."

Another participant discloses: "I confronted my own death. When I fell, it was real. And then to be reborn and to die and to be reborn and to die again also felt real. When I live with the fact of my death, every moment is more important and I value my life more. I don't have time to fool around and waste my life on inconsequential matters."

I seek to make scores that are responsive to both the needs of the performers and the themes of the dance. There are some difficulties, however, in translating real-life issues into a movement score. One of the problems has to do with time and the different ways that time unfolds in a ritual context, a workshop context, and a performance context. Many years ago my friend Norma Leistiko was participating in an evening dance session in which we explored "mineral" as a movement resource. She chose "rock" and became so totally immersed in this experience that she remained in a still position for the entire three-hour class. I left the studio without disturbing Norma, assuming she would soon come out of her rock image and leave for home. To my surprise and amazement, when I went to the studio the next morning, I found her in the same position as when I had left. She had been a rock all night.

I myself try dancing the Rising and Falling score during the workshop. I invent numerous ways to fall and rise that conjure up many meaningful images around the theme of life and death. I hesitate going more deeply into the falling part of the score because I am afraid I may not rise again for hours, as happened with Norma when she became a rock. I become so concerned about the score that I cannot surrender to the experience itself. Part of my difficulty has to do with my role as the teacher. It just isn't appropriate for me to go fully into my own experience while I am guiding others through theirs. But another part of my difficulty is my need for an amount of time that just isn't realistic.

This highlights one of the problems with the ritual dances I am trying to create. I want everything to be real and to reflect our authentic experiences, but decisions about time continue to be compromises. Our preconceptions of dance shape our notion of time within it—either we have to get out of the building by a certain time or we have to limit our activities for the sake of the audience. In *Circle the Earth*, the way we do the Earth Run is an example of this compromise. When we do it on the mountain and there are no viewers or time limit, we may run for a long time. When we do it with witnesses in a theater setting, it always ends in relationship to how long it sustains the viewers' interest. These concerns are real, but not conducive to the work itself or to the principles governing a ritual. I have not overcome this limitation, and I continue to long for a dance unencumbered by time restrictions. I would like *Circle the Earth* to be a true ritual, but I believe it is merely a performance with ritual principles until it defies this problem of theatrical time.

FINDING COMMUNITY VALUES
THROUGH VALUACTION

The Rising and Falling score creates many different reactions, some quite heated. The way we work together as a group comes into focus as we discuss and valuact the score. Several people underline their difficulties with carrying out the actions of falling or rising. One person says, "I felt a strong resistance against falling. I didn't like it. I was glad to stand on the ground and feel my feet." Another comments, "For me, rising up was like reaching for something. I had to break through a wall just to see something, to grow up. But it was easy to fall down."

Many describe strong emotions. "I found myself experiencing a tremendous amount of sadness and pain," acknowledges one participant. "At the same time, I was longing for freedom from it. I wanted to get through it. I wanted a moment of everybody standing up." Another admits, "I was frightened at the beginning when some people began to rise and some people didn't move at all. I had this momentary panic that the people who didn't move weren't going to move, that they were just going to lie there."

A polarity in the group is noticed. Some have a desire for everything to be perfect, while others dwell on the struggle of existence. How can we find common ground in this field of differences? When we turn to a discussion of how the score might end, the opposing perspectives are clearly represented. "I would love to see everyone standing up, as opposed to down," one person declares. "I think down is giving in to death. By everyone standing up, we're fighting for life because it's worth it." But another person counters, "We're all individuals and we all have our own paths. It has to be wherever you are. We're up and down throughout life. I can't imagine standing up at the end if that's not where I am at that moment."

This kind of dialogue is important to me. It establishes our community values, which are relevant in the creation of a dance of this sort. The group finally comes to a consensus that supports each individual's attitude and right to choose, while maintaining membership in the collective by following the score. It is decided that whatever statement is made has to include everyone's input. During our discussion, we address the following questions in positive and affirming ways: Who am I? Who are we? What are our values? These are important questions to ask as we create community myths.

LEARNING HOW TO GIVE FEEDBACK

A key part of the Rising and Falling score is learning how to witness and give feedback. Being a witness is different from being an audience member. A witness participates by watching and then sharing her experience of what she saw. An audience member tends to come to the theater to be entertained, and her only shared response may be applause (if that). Both in the workshop and in the performance we encourage a connection between witnesses and performers that deepens the experience for everyone. No one is outside the circle of the performance: the dancers do it for themselves and the witnesses; the witnesses watch it for themselves and to support the dancers.

One participant describes being riveted when witnessing M's performance: "She was kicking and squirming to get born. I resented her! I couldn't share my feelings, but I was sitting next to someone who said exactly what I wanted to say." M's performance was highly individualized and emotionally charged, but the feedback she receives suggests that the witness doesn't approve. M doesn't respond verbally in the big group discussion, but when she performs a second time, she is visibly less enthusiastic and her performance lacks the "juice" of the first time. Later, in her small support group, she reports that she was hurt by the criticism and couldn't perform with full commitment.

This example illustrates how potentially damaging criticism can be to creativity when feedback is unstructured and allowed to lapse into judgment. Praise can be damaging as well, if it leads others to make comparisons and find themselves lacking. In addition, if you are told that what you did was wonderful and amazing (i.e., "good"), you may fall into a trap of always repeating the same patterns, even when they are no longer alive for you. Learning to give feedback that enhances creativity is crucial to the process of creating a dance like *Circle the Earth*. When feedback is directed toward the expansion of our creativity, rather than its repression, we become allies for one another. Reporting your visceral or emotional responses as a witness can be useful, as long as they're communicated in a nonjudgmental way. The preferred language to use when giving this kind of feedback is, "When I saw you do that, I felt ...," rather than "What you did was amazing (or scary or . . .)." Being a responsible witness is different from being a critic. It involves giving the performer an understanding of how he or she has affected you without adding value judgments. Unlike feedback that comes from preconceived ideas or external standards, this kind of feedback can open up dialogue between the witness and the performer. When we give each other a window into our subjective experiences of each other's performances, what we communicate is a piece of our own humanity, rather than our capacity to judge or separate ourselves from each other. This helps us break down our personal isolation and practice making genuine connections with one another.

Learning how to give feedback is part of establishing a safe environment for all participants. It's up to the workshop leader to state the directions and parameters of the score for valuactions, and to objectively define the differences between constructive and destructive comments. One way to do this is to focus on whether the performers followed the score and whether the score generated creativity. It is also important to distinguish between nonjudgmental and judgmental feedback by using examples and giving people permission to speak when they feel criticized or judged. In general, participants need to be encouraged to talk about their own perceptions, rather than to evaluate someone else's performance. Remind people to concentrate on feedback that reflects their own kinesthetic and emotional states. What did you see? What touched or affected you? Were there any images that came up? These are all good questions for witnesses to answer as they give feedback.

At this stage in the workshop, people's differences are vital resources that, when made visible, can be useful to everybody. When people's differences are responded to with judgment, it becomes difficult for people to express themselves. It is especially important to monitor for this in a multicultural group, where there can be so many unconscious ways for people in more powerful cultural positions to dominate those in less powerful positions. To invite everyone to the dialogue, we need to carefully check our cultural biases at the door.

VISUALIZATION

After the Rising and Falling score and its valuaction, I ask participants to draw their images of life and death. Afterward, we share these visualizations with our support groups. We try to answer the questions: What does your visualization say to you? How does it connect to your life and your dance? As with other visualization scores, the results are unique, and the sharing that takes place after the drawing results in further connections among participants and a greater sense of the larger myth through which the group functions. The intention of this score is to cultivate a greater understanding of our theme and to deepen our empathy for one another.

CLOSURE

To close our work for the day I offer a score that gives participants a chance to connect with one another and acknowledge the different ways they have related to one another during the day.

Intention:	Integrate the experiences of the day.
SCORE	
Time:	1 hour.
Space:	Entire space.
People:	All participants, in large group and then in support groups.

Activities:

1. Form a large circle.
2. Take time to look at each other.

Identifying the Central Theme

Here are some questions to consider:

What central theme is related to your community's issue?

What kind of movement score might embody this theme? Does it, for example, relate to rising and falling?

What kind of warm-up is most appropriate for your group?

How can you create a safe container, allowing people to talk with one another about how the dance is impacting them?

How can you guide participants to really listen to one another's experiences and concerns without offering judgment?

When you need support as a leader, is there someone you can turn to?

Are your designated support people for the workshop connecting with the dancers?

Do you check in regularly with your facilitators to make sure everybody's being taken care of?

Are you sure that both the participants and the facilitators are getting the support they need in order to keep the emotional flow of the dance moving?

---

3. Go to someone you've had a strong experience with and make nonverbal contact.
4. Write in your journal.
5. Go to your support group and share what you've written in your journal and what your experience has been.

Some participants underline what the Rising and Falling score means in terms of their ongoing lives. One woman stresses that she doesn't have any time to waste. "I could die any minute," she says. "I want to live fully and experience every moment. I don't want to pass up any opportunities to love people and to ask for their love and to connect in a very deep way." Other participants simply voice how glad they are to have had the chance to spend a whole day with one another, in their bodies, taking time to look at their relationship to life and death.

A BUILDING TENSION

In the support groups, some participants express a feeling that they are divided into "haves" and "have-nots." One young man stands up and says that he feels alienated because the people who are HIV-positive are the stars of the show and are getting all the attention. A shocked silence follows this outrageous remark. One HIV-positive member of the group tells him quite explicitly, "Please, if you want it, take it. I will gladly give it up!" There is nervous laughter, but at the same time we know something important has been said.

I am concerned about the polarizing tension around the issue of inclusion or exclusion, and I know that no amount of talking will resolve this crucial conflict. I want to find a way to use this situation as a creative resource and generate a new score of resolution. That night at home, I ponder the gravity of the group's position. All the lovely peace and harmony I imagined was building in the group has been shattered, and instead I feel only a smoldering discontent. We have only a few days to pull the entire piece together; I am afraid that we will be destroyed by this conflict. It has to be resolved—now.

This type of high-pressure situation underlines for me the challenges of a theater of realism—when such raw human experiences emerge, they call for immediate resolution through new and creative means. I put aside the self-doubt that comes to me at times like these (as well as the real questions about my sanity in taking on such a presumptuous project in the first place), and get to work creating a score to deal with the situation. The score we need must be simple because of our time constraints. In addition to simplicity, the score needs to risk exposing the nature of the conflict itself. And I know from experience that embodying the issue is going to be more effective than further dialogue among group members. Together with the Reverend Sandy Winter, my consultant, I design a new score—"I Want to Live!"—which we will try out at the end of the next day.

DAY 4. *Preparing to Confront the Dark Side*

This day is devoted to readying ourselves to confront the dark side. We start with a score that allows us to connect with our bodies and each other. This is a variation of the "tune-up" score that we use each day, focusing on different skills at different times—accentuating the up- or downbeat, finding relaxation in the energetic movements, or cultivating a sense of wildness. Today, I am particularly interested in energizing and mobilizing people's bodies and getting everyone to explore different spatial paths and levels.

TUNING IN TO THE BODY PULSE

Intention: Prepare us to work with unison movement.

Teach techniques for rhythmic and spatial awareness.

SCORE

Time: 1 hour or more.

Space: Entire space.

People: All participants.

Activities:

1. Spread throughout the space in small clusters, standing by yourself next to others.
2. Pulse in place, vibrating with the drumbeat, until you feel the energy moving through your entire body. Play with the movement, repeating it over and over until you "lose your head and come to your senses," as Fritz Perls would say.
3. Allow the pulse to take you into a walk through the space and begin to interact with other people.
4. When the leader spontaneously shouts out a spatial direction or formation (e.g., circle, tunnel, cluster, diagonal line), respond as quickly as possible.
5. Return to pulsing and walking until the leader calls out another direction. The leader may add different levels: up, down, etc.
6. Repeat a number of times.
7. Form two lines facing each other and create a unison movement.

One purpose of this score is to prepare participants for the stomping movements of the next score, which introduces the Warrior movement.

INTRODUCTION TO THE WARRIOR MOVEMENT

The Warrior Dance will become a forceful moment in the performance of *Circle the Earth*. It involves the deliberate use of really large body movements, done in unison and in straight lines across the space. It emphasizes the power of the moment when we are preparing to drive the dark side of AIDS and HIV into the light. We practice this several times in the workshop, to touch that part of ourselves that provides support and stability against our demons, both in ourselves and those we love.

Three considerations go into the selection of the Warrior movement. First, it has to have a steady, insistent, and repetitive beat. This is an affirmation of the Warrior's determination. Second, the largest muscles of the body are chosen to express this posture. The Warrior movement for the lower body consists of a repetitive high-stepping movement that alter-

Anna in Warrior stance. Photo © Paul Fusco/ Magnum Photos.

nates from right to left leg. It involves lifting one leg to the side and, with a strong downbeat, letting it fall in a stomping gesture. To coordinate with the lower body movement, the chest resists and rises up rather than down, allowing you to emit a loud sound as the leg pounds down. Using large movements that activate so much of the body engages a sense of commitment. In addition, the face takes on a Warrior's stance: the nostrils flare, the lower jaw juts forward, the upper lip curls, exposing the teeth, and the eyes flash to accentuate each down-step.

It is important that each dancer discover within these movements an expression of his or her individual experience, rather than merely offering an external illustration. I choose these movements because doing them can give participants an experience of affirmative aggressive power. But to be effective, the person must respond internally to the experience of being a Warrior. If the dancers are only imitating the movement as opposed to feeling it internally, it will be apparent. When participants viscerally experience the Warrior movement, there is a marked visual change. Some people may shy away at first and have a difficult time entering the dance. However, because the content and form of the movement are so congruent in this dance, someone who is afraid or timid in the beginning may be able to overcome this initial emotion. It is precisely because of its transformative quality that I chose this particular movement. To help activate this dance inside us, we also take the time to draw an image of our Warrior.

Intention: Gain strength to confront the dark side.

SCORE

Time: 1 hour (or more, depending on group size).

Space: Entire space.

People: All participants.

Activities:

1. After the leader demonstrates, try out the Warrior movement.
2. Continue practicing, with drums used to reinforce the movement.
3. Divide into two or more lines, linking arms and moving forward and back in space while doing the Warrior movement in unison.
4. After practicing the Warrior movement, draw an image of your Warrior. Write down what you imagine your Warrior is saying.
5. Share your drawing with a partner in your support group. Take time to dance the drawing, using the Warrior movement, with your partner as witness.

One man, who has the HIV virus, is blocking the fear and anxiety he feels. He looks at his Warrior image, which shows a large and muscular body with red legs and arms. When he tries to dance it, his legs are shaky at first and he simply can't begin. Then his partner repeats the words he has written on his drawing—"I fear thee not"—over and over again as he lifts and stomps his legs. These words and encouragement have an effect on him. Finally, the movement, the emotion, the language, and the image lead him to an experience of being a powerful Warrior combating the destructive force of his distress and his terror of HIV. He begins to move with powerful strides, embodying his Warrior in a deeper way. As the movement influences his emotions, the dance changes the dancer.

Sometimes we do scores that match our emotions, but just as important are scores that don't. In this case, the participant's Warrior drawing did not match his emotions, but dancing his drawing eventually transformed them.

GUIDED VISUALIZATION: FINDING A SAFE PLACE

Before we plunge into the dark side of the anger, fear, and anguish associated with a life-threatening struggle, it is imperative to secure three things: a safe and strong place within, a way to maintain yourself through the darkness, and a place to which you can return. A guided visualization directs participants to find a place in nature where they want to be, a place that offers healing. The place can be anywhere in the world, real or imaginary. Participants imagine themselves in this environment, taking it in with all their senses. After they experience this place, they are asked to draw a picture of it. Then these pictures are shared in support groups. This process helps participants locate a harmonious and protective relationship to nature within their own bodies, so that after confronting the dark side they will be able to return to themselves for the kind of nourishment we get from the natural world.

Intention: Find a restorative resting place inside oneself.
SCORE
Time: 1 hour.
Space: Entire space.
People: All participants.
Activities:

1. Lie down and relax, closing your eyes and listening to your breathing.
2. The leader guides participants: "Imagine a place in nature where you want to be. A place that is serene, peaceful, inspiring, and healing. It can be somewhere you've been before or somewhere you imagine. See yourself resting alone with no obligations, worries, or concerns. There is nothing you have to do. Enjoy this place—its smells, noises, colors, feel, and sights. All your senses are alive, your mind is free. Every cell in your body radiates a sense of health, peace, and love."
3. When you are ready, draw this place and yourself in it.

This visualization provides an opportunity for workshop participants to gather a resource that will be useful as a place to return to after they actually confront their monsters. Participants are vulnerable in this confrontation and need a safe, protective, and reassuring place to restore them.

LIFTING SCORE

It's important that participants be ready and able to facilitate restoration after we go into the dark side. To help build a sense of trust in each other, we teach participants how to lift a passive person from a lying to a sitting to a standing position.

Intention: Learn to lift effortlessly.

Provide physical experience of support.

SCORE

Time: 30 minutes.

Space: Scattered in room.

People: All participants, in partners (one active, one passive).

Activities:

1. Passive partner: lie down on your back while the active partner sits.
2. Active partner: lift your passive partner by the back of the head to a sitting position.
3. Passive partner: remain passive, but cooperative. When you are lifted to sitting, stay in that position.
4. Active partner: stand facing your passive partner and hold your partner by the wrists, then bring your partner to standing simply by taking several steps backward.
5. Switch roles and repeat.

In this day's workshop we also introduce two additional restoration resources, both of which will be used in the performance: the Restoration Song and the Bridge (see "Release and Restoration" in day 9). We then ask participants to share their drawings of their restorative resting places with their support groups and to talk about their highs and lows, as well as their needs and wants.

"I WANT TO LIVE!"

At the end of the day we try out the score developed to address the tension expressed in earlier valuations, between those who are living with the AIDS virus and those who are not. The idea is to find a common intention that everybody can carry into the creation of the dance performance.

Intention: Express our connection to life.

Alleviate the polarization of the group.

SCORE

Time: Individual timing.

Space: Two lines with a path between them.

People: Each participant separately.

Activities:

1. Form a path of people lining either side of the space.
2. Starting from the back, run or walk down the path one by one and declare, "I want to live!"

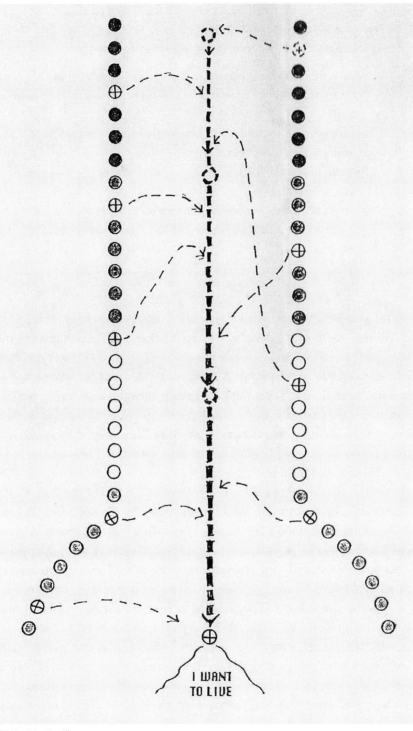

"I Want to Live!" score.

Preparing to Confront the Dark Side

As you approach fear-inducing issues, consider these questions:

What is the dark side associated with your community's theme?

What kind of resources do your participants need to confront the dark side?

Is there a movement resource like the Warrior stance that will build strength for the confrontation?

How can you establish a safe place that each member of your group can return to?

Are there additional movement skills that participants need to learn beforehand to facilitate release and restoration after confronting the dark side?

This score engenders many reactions. Some people resist doing it at all. All the HIV-positive people participate. Some caregivers change the words to "I am alive." Some people run and leap joyously. Others run with determination or quiet power. As one man later recalls, "When it was my turn, when I said, 'I want to live,' I really meant it. It wasn't a performance. It wasn't a dance. It was the first time in my life I consciously said, 'I want to live.' And it was the first time since I had been diagnosed with AIDS, I consciously said 'I want to live' and meant it. This was the most powerful moment for me."

I am the next to last person. When I get to the end of the line, I turn around and begin shouting, "And I want you to live!" and I call each person by name. In that moment, I understand what this dance means to me and why I am doing it. It isn't just that I want to live. I want the people I love to live with me. One woman summarizes the healing potential of the score: "I think healing people with AIDS is not a momentary process. It's ongoing. I think it's about healing everyone—everyone's anger and fear and shut-down feelings. And every time someone cries and someone else holds them, every time someone moves and dances and is really committed to it, there's a healing. When Anna turned back to everyone and said, 'I want you to live,' she said my name and the names of people I love who are here. It's the deepest respect, the deepest kind of love to say, 'I want you to live.'"

Afterward the group makes a circle, holds each other, and cries. The score has a profound effect on the whole group and helps us find our compassion, courage, and strength. The circle of fear, death, and isolation is breaking; a circle of trust, support, and community healing is forming. In the brief, intense minutes it takes to perform this score, the group discovers a way to state its own specific intention for *Dancing with Life on the Line*. What has seemed like a barrier between people begins to take on a new shape. It begins to look, instead, like a bond.

"I Want to Live!" identifies the issue of life and death, the central theme of the entire dance. The process of identification is crucial in the healing process. We have found our commonality—we all want to live. The direct personal experience of the group, as well as the experience of living with HIV, coalesces in this score to create what will be one of the most emotionally charged moments of the entire dance. The group discovers its common theme through the score, and the conflict is resolved through dance. It shows the effectiveness of using a movement score, an embodying situation, to creatively deal with a real-life issue in a large group. The group could have resolved its differences through verbal discussion, but it would have taken a good deal of time and facilitation and may have led to more confusion. The movement score goes right to the core issue of the group.

DAY 5. *Releasing the Dark Side*

After identifying the central issue of the dance, dancing together, and discovering the meaningful relationships among us, we now are a powerful, motivated, and unified group ready to confront the dark side. This is a pivotal point in the workshop, as well as a pivotal point in the healing process. I feel confident that this group has what it needs to make this confrontation—we have not only the intensity of our struggle for life, but we have also connected with our capacity to repair and restore ourselves and our relationships.

In developing this section of our work together, I look for the most extreme and intense images and movements to help us gain access to this deep place inside ourselves. What I now call the Mask or Monster Dance grew out of this challenge. In addition to our usual body-tuning warm-up, we engage in some simple scores that sensitize our bodies, as well as activating feelings of intimacy, vulnerability, and trust.

TOUCH AND BODY CONTOUR SCORES

Intention: Build sensitivity and receptivity to touch.
SCORE
Time: Open.

Space: Spread out in room.

People: All participants, in partners.

Activities:

1. Lie on the floor and relax.
2. Open your mouth and yawn. Make sounds from the yawn.
3. Touch your body and yawn.
4. Find a partner and sit facing each other, making eye contact with a soft focus, taking care not to stare invasively.
5. One person: touch your partner. Partner: receive the touch. Switch roles.
6. Explore touching and being touched using different parts of your body.
7. Add lying down and standing as options and explore contouring your body to your partner's body. One partner: make contact while the other receives. Alternate roles.

This score can also be done with participants sitting in two concentric circles. After everyone performs the score with the person she or he is initially facing, the dancers in the inner circle move one person to the left, so each is facing someone new. The score's activities are then repeated.

It is important with this score to request that participants use sensitivity about where to touch their partners. Obviously, any contact construed as sexual is not welcome and should not be sanctioned. Everyone should be encouraged to build sensitivity to others as they use the powerful resource of touch.

THE POWER OF A MASK

Masks have been worn throughout history in every part of the world. They have been created with a range of materials by the old and the young, by skilled artists and ordinary people, for utilitarian purposes, entertainment, worship, and magic. Some of the most impressive and evocative masks have been used for religious or sacred ceremonies and represent ancestors, gods, or spirits. The person wearing the mask is often regarded as the impersonation of the spirit and is, at least temporarily, aligned with the power of the supernatural. A mask is a container for the spirit. When you put a mask on, you call that spirit into your body and you become that spirit.

In Bali, where almost every dance is done with a mask, the mask dancer has a very important role. The dances evoke the spirit world that is an integral part of the Balinese culture. Through dance, music, and narration, the dancers enact the myths of their culture, and these dances help maintain the continuity, values, and spiritual life of the community. When I was in Bali, I stopped in a village where I followed a procession to an open courtyard in front of a temple. The dancers and villagers were in the midst of a festival. In the center of the courtyard was a magnificently decorated altar and on the altar were three huge, elaborate masks. One was the Destroyer, another the Creator, and the third the Protector. These are the three central characters of the Balinese Hindu pantheon, and a dancer embodies the spirit of the particular mask when performing the dance. Among other things, this Balinese dance is one of exorcism and renewal, a dance that needs to be done over and over again, year after year, as a way to sustain the culture of the community.

What I found especially fascinating was the universality of the three characters in this dance. The Destroyer is similar to what I call the Monster in *Circle the Earth*, the Protector is like the Warrior, and the Creator is the Restorer. In the Balinese dance that I saw, the Destroyer went into a deep state of trance; when he finished, two people stayed at his side until he was ready to reenter the ordinary world again. In *Circle the Earth*, those who restore the Monsters take on a similar role. When I was in the Balinese village, I could not communicate with the people in words, but I felt a deep kinship with them and their rituals. I imagined that our two communities would have understood each other even though our dances look very different. Theirs is a highly stylized form that has been refined over hundreds of years, while ours involves a simple and direct use of unrefined movement newly invented and almost raw by comparison. Yet the intent and even the spirit of the dances seem the same. I went away from the village feeling humbled, inspired, and intimately connected to some larger universal spirit.

MOLDING THE FACE

Each part of the body has a primary function and unique qualities of expression. The face is the site of speech, sound, sight, hearing, and smell. It is how we feed ourselves, and it is one of the focal points for communication. The importance of facial signals is deeply embedded in our language; for example, "poker-face," "two-faced," "saving face," and "facing up to it" are common expressions in English. Upon rising, we brush our teeth, wash our faces, and comb our hair before venturing out into the world. We don't usually look at our feet or the backs of our legs. We look at the face. It is the face that gives us the most insight into another's state of mind. Because it is such a highly charged area and sends such strong signals, we learn to control it in order to present—or mask—our thoughts and emotions.

Every society has rules of social communication with specific boundaries, and the face is formed and held in ways conditioned by those rules. Uncensored by those rules, the face also holds deeply buried imprints stored in the body. The face holds memories and thoughts that are taboo, old emotions that have been blocked, suppressed, or never expressed. Those blockages can in turn cut off energy fields, causing a great disharmony.

We each have our own characteristic "game face," one we have held onto for so many years that we are unconscious of its expression. This is the face we use to approach daily life. When we disrupt our unconscious expressions by purposefully altering the face, we tap into deeply buried emotions. How often have you smiled to hide anger or even tears? We can alter the face in ways that create a mask so frightening it both demands and enables a confrontation with the destructive forces inside us. Disgust, anger, rage, frustration, powerlessness, self-hate, sadness, grief, and shame may suddenly emerge as the face is explored and altered. Prepare to be surprised, shocked, or even amused by what may be revealed.

Intention: Evoke and confront the destructive forces within us. Reveal the truth behind the mask.

SCORE

Time: 1 hour.

Space: Entire space.

People: All participants, each with a partner.

Activities:

1. Sit down with your partner and face each other.
2. Using your fingers, mold your partner's face. Passive partner: allow the active partner to change the contours of your face.
3. Once your face (as the passive partner) is altered, freeze your facial muscles into a "mask." Notice what emotions are aroused from the expression frozen on your face.
4. Allow this face to become the impetus for movement of your whole body. Pay attention to your emotions and images.
5. Rest and share your experience with your partner.
6. Switch roles.

DRAWING AND DANCING A MASK

Once new facial expressions have been revealed to us, it is important to personalize this experience, and to draw and dance the mask that feels the most specific to our situation, that hides our worst fears or holds a particular authority and power for us. The embodiment of this mask often sends the participant into a deep place, one that is rarely expressed in public, or even to oneself. It is this mask that often shields us from the part of the world that terrifies or threatens us.

Intention: Face your destructive forces.

SCORE

Time: 2 hours.

Space: Entire space.

People: All participants, alone and with a partner.

Activities:

1. Draw a mask that feels most connected to your dark side.
2. On the drawing, write a statement that best expresses what the mask is saying to you. What do you want to confront and release?
3. Give your drawing to your partner to hold, then take a position directly across the room.
4. Turn your back to your partner (and the mask) and find a centered place inside yourself.
5. Turn around to face your partner, who is holding your drawing up for you to see. As you turn, transform your face into the mask you have drawn and make sounds that connect you to it.
6. Keep the mask movements concentrated in your face and dance toward your drawing.
7. When you reach your partner, release the mask in your face and relax into the floor.
8. Breathe. In your mind, picture the peaceful place in nature that you drew the preceding day.
9. Partner: place a hand on some part of the mask dancer's body and feel the breath. When breathing has begun to return to normal, help your partner sit up and then stand.
10. Rest as needed before changing roles and repeating the score.
11. Take time to share verbally with your partner your experience of dancing and witnessing this score.

Ordinarily, in a dance performance, we might cover the face with a mask to create a certain image. This is certainly visually effective, but it makes for an entirely different kind of performance than the one we are creating in *Circle the Earth*. Instead of covering our faces with masks, we form our own masks with our faces. We aren't putting on masks to cover ourselves up; rather, we are creating masks that express emotions

Drawing the Monster mask. Photo © Christine Anderson.

Partners holding Monster masks as participants dance toward them. Photo © Kathy Straus.

The power of the mask as a way of both confronting destructive forces and providing protection is evident among the indigenous Andaman people, who live on an island in the Indian Ocean. Each year, they reenact a stunning myth and ritual. The story is as follows: A man with a frightening, violent mask appears from the village's lake in a canoe, shouting and screaming. All the villagers are frightened. They race to their homes, lock the doors, and close the windows. The masked man rages through the village and finally disappears, promising that he'll be back next year. One year the villagers get together and decide they will all make the same mask this man wears and run to the water's edge, screaming and howling, as the masked man canoes toward them. The stranger arrives in his canoe as usual, but when he sees the villagers wearing these monstrous masks he becomes so frightened he falls overboard and drowns. Afterward the evil spirit does not come back, but every year the villagers enact this ritual to remember to face their fears and be alert enough to come together as a community to protect themselves from danger.

we often cover up in our daily lives. The contracting of facial muscles triggers movements that express the emotions inherent in the mask image. The performer is not pretending, but simultaneously enacting the mask image and experiencing its influence. This enactment is so real that performers can actually experience the fear, stress, anger, frustration, anxiety, or disgust that the dark side holds for them. The mask is a symbol of each participant's confrontation with the dark side; by enacting and dancing the mask, these destructive forces can be released.

One participant remembers looking at his mask drawing and seeing "eyes that were burning red with yellow and green, and a mouth that was a block of intense red, lined and ricocheting the color black in all directions." As his partner held up this drawing, he recalls, "I gathered all of the strength I could muster in order to be able to release all the feelings I had toward the virus, 'my enemy.' As I moved across the floor, I embodied the rage I was feeling. Upon reaching my portrait, I ripped it right out of the holder's hands. I wanted to destroy it for the sake of my own survival."

The very act of drawing a mask can raise confrontational issues. One participant, for example, doesn't want to draw a mask. Instead, he draws generalized lines, colors, and shapes. Yet I still feel that this drawing will help him. He describes what he has drawn as "a black hole" and says he is disappearing in it. We explore this and discover that he relates this to his

---

Releasing the Dark Side

In facing the dark side that may be tied to your community's issue, consider these questions:

Is there a mask that is covering over a highly charged issue? And, if so, what kinds of emotions are hidden by this mask?

Have you provided enough resources on the previous day to prepare people to confront their monsters?

Have you established a strong sense of support within the group so that participants can hold themselves and one another through this process?

Are your facilitators adequately trained to respond to participants' emotional reactions?

---

resignation toward dying. He begins to pour out his sense of worthlessness, how it won't matter if he disappears. I ask him who he is talking to. He says, "The people out there." After talking some more about the people out there, he finally tells me that he is a good gardener and a good dancer. He gets more in touch with himself until he is ready to draw a real mask. I suggest he draw a mask that will drive the "people out there" away, and drive the virus out of his body.

Making the choice "not to disappear" becomes this participant's theme throughout the workshop and performance. In situation after situation, he chooses to make himself highly visible, charging out first in our public performance of the Monster Dance. Through the drawing and dancing of his mask, he finds new strength and determination to fight for his life. He later says, "What I finally came to is that I can look at my dark side, the mask, and still be the one in control. So that if the virus is there, I can live with the virus. As long as the virus knows that I'm the one that's in control. I spent a lot of time really fighting it and wanting to be out of my body, but that's not realistic for me and where I'm at right now. The virus is in my body, that's a reality. I've accepted that. What it's about for me now is saying that I'm the one who is in control of my body, not the virus."

As a preliminary restoration after such a highly charged confrontation, I encourage participants to do a simple score where they gently mold their own faces to restore a sense of calm and peace. It's important for them to take responsibility for this initial restoration themselves, to experience their own ability to soothe themselves.

DAY 6. *Recovery*

The intention for this day is to offer more time to recover from the intensity of confronting the dark side and to arrive at a more balanced state, relating to others in the group in a supportive way. Relating to each other through touch in a noninvasive manner is a delicate and essential skill we need to ensure trust and safety. It is important to know how to place your hands on another person's body in a nonsexual way. For example, shaking hands is an act of friendship. Touching with the palm of the hand can be healing and soothing. Touching lightly with the head can be tender; touching fully with the back can be supporting—I am backing you up. We all know that in ordinary life physical touch is a powerful language. By bringing awareness to how to use touch in a caring way, we can gain insights into how we relate to each other and to the larger community. I've developed a process that allows people to experiment with their awareness of touch and the various possible ways of relating to others.

We begin by working in partners, shaking hands, saying hello, tapping shoulders, placing our palms on one another's backs to feel the breath, and then transition into a tune-up score with energizing movements, interacting freely and practicing coming together by moving to a common beat, as we do in the Vortex Dance. Afterward, we sit down as a group for a valuaction, providing an opportunity for feedback. We want to know if there is anything more we can do to ensure the sense of a safe and protected environment. The rest of the day is spent exploring how we relate to others, as a way of deepening our sense of community.

ACTIVE/PASSIVE SCORE

To uncover the different roles we may play in our relationships, we try out different degrees of active and passive movement (see the chart later in this section). The Active/Passive score gives us a chance to investigate our individual mythologies as well as to build new ways of relating to each other.

Intention:	Experience different degrees of activity or passivity in relation to another person.
SCORE	
Time:	2 hours.
Space:	Entire space.
People:	All participants, in partners.

Activities:

Part I. Lying Passive

1. Decide who will be passive first. Passive person: lie down, eyes closed, and allow your partner to manipulate your body. Active person: sit near your partner's head, with your eyes open.

2. Active partner: begin to work on your partner's head, using gentle movements. Holding it lightly with both hands, rock it very slowly from side to side. Lift your partner's head slowly, then place it softly on the ground. Explore different pivoting, lateral, and flexing movements, but avoid the tendency to massage your partner, as that diffuses the experience.

3. Pause, then move quietly to your partner's side and begin to lift an arm. If your partner seems unable to let go, hold still and softly encourage your partner to release the arm's weight, saying, "Breathe out and let go."

4. Explore different movements, lifting the arm, rotating it, gently shaking it, moving it across the body or overhead. Manipulate the arm by holding it just above the wrist joint or just below the elbow joint.

5. Notice if other parts of your partner's body freely follow the arm's movement (for example, if you gently pull the arm, the shoulder and neck often follow). Also notice if your partner's body doesn't follow, but do not force anyone's body to do anything it isn't ready to do.

6. Before changing to the other arm, ask your partner to notice any difference in sensation between one arm and the other.

7. Repeat steps 3–5 with the other arm.

8. Do similar explorations with each leg. Then rest.

9. Passive partner: take several minutes to explore your own movements, drawing on what you have just experienced.

10. Take a few minutes to give feedback to each other. Were there ways your partner touched you that helped you let go? Did anything feel uncomfortable, making it difficult to let go? Was the speed OK or did your partner move too fast, setting up resistance?

11. Switch roles.

There are many variations on this exercise. One variation is to use a towel, rather than your hands, so that the touch remains as objective as possible. Human touch often carries hidden and distracting messages.

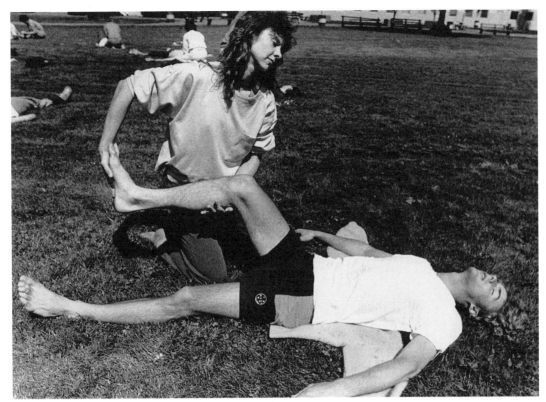

Passive/active exercise. Photo © Christine Anderson.

Part II. Letting Yourself Be Led

1. Both partners sit facing each other. Passive partner: close your eyes and place your hands on top of the active partner's palms.
2. Active partner: with eyes open, use your hands to move your partner in different directions. Avoid moving the hands so far that you put the passive partner off balance. Passive partner: Let yourself go with the movement—don't initiate it, but don't resist it.
3. When told, switch roles.

When you are in a sitting position, your relationship to gravity shifts so that you can no longer be completely passive. The active person in this part of the score is the initiator of the movement, with the passive person as a follower.

Part III. Letting Yourself Be Moved Through Space

1. Find a new partner. Stand and face each other. Passive partner: put your hands on the active partner's palms and close your eyes.
2. Active partner: with eyes open, lead your partner into whole

body movements. Stay essentially in place, but experiment with changing levels, direction, speed (but not too fast), and the like.

3. Active partner: now slowly move your partner through space. Be aware of everything around you, to avoid losing your partner's trust by bumping into other people. If you notice your partner holding her or his breath, slow down.

4. Experiment with different qualities of movement, always carefully observing the impact of your leadership.

5. When you feel your partner is secure with you, begin to lead with just one hand, releasing the other hand.

6. Sometimes release both hands, allowing your partner to come into stillness.

7. Try moving your partner with parts of your body other than your hands. This is an opportunity to create a beautiful and expressive dance with your partner.

8. Switch roles.

This score stimulates a variety of reactions. Moving under the direction of an outside force without being able to control your own movements can be exciting, comforting, or frightening, for example. I have seen people hold their breath with anxiety while being led or unconsciously stiffen their bodies in fear. They feel they are losing control. For this reason, it is important to begin slowly, with care and gentleness, and to observe your partner's responses, adjusting the way you lead accordingly. Some people prefer being led, while others prefer leading. Some like both equally. In my life as a teacher, I have done a lot of leading. I like to turn the situation around and let myself be led sometimes. I am excited by the unpredictability of movement as well as the comfort of someone else taking the initiative to create my movements.

With concentration and practice, this is an effective exercise to cultivate trust in one's own kinesthetic capacities, to increase one's experiences of qualities and types of movements you would not ordinarily choose to do. It also helps dissolve habitual patterns. For the one leading, this exercise can cultivate an ability to witness other people, to develop confidence in taking the initiative, and to develop an awareness of how speed, dynamics, and uses of space can generate feelings and emotional reactions.

Now that we have established the two different roles, the next step is to begin to blend these two roles in unpredictable and spontaneous ways.

A basic template for understanding our roles in relationships can be viewed in the following way:

Partner 1	Partner 2
Active	Active
Active	Passive
Passive	Active
Passive	Passive

This chart illustrates a variety of scoring possibilities. Exploring these relationships can create some very unexpected, exciting, and even funny connections. Imagine two people wanting to lead at the same time or one partner going suddenly passive, or both partners going passive. Trained dancers can use the Active/Passive score to generate new movement experiences, and untrained dancers may also find themselves moving in surprising new ways. The drama inherent in this score has far-reaching potential.

If time permits, the score can be further developed to reflect on real-life relationships. You might ask yourself: What is my dance in life with my primary relationship? Am I always in one role, active or passive? What do I want more of? Less of? Create a score of what your relationship is now. Next, create a score of what you would like it to be. Ask other people to perform your scores so that you can be a witness. You may be amused, saddened, or surprised when you witness the outcome. This simple movement score applied to our real-life experiences is an example of the Life/Art Process.

Part IV. Shifting between Active and Passive

1. Choose a new partner. Both dancers: keep your eyes open and make some kind of body contact with each other.
2. Without determining in advance who will be active and who will be passive, begin to move together. Imagine a scale going from 1 (completely passive) to 10 (completely active), and experiment with different degrees on this scale.

Two people may be relatively passive at the same time, creating a soft, empathetic dance. Or both partners may be active, leading to pushing, pulling, falling, and other kinds of energetic, oppositional movements. There can be sudden shifts from an active/active relationship to an active/

passive one. This can change the whole scope of the dance, leading to such actions as carrying, dragging, or lifting.

The Active/Passive score can deepen our understanding of the roles we take in our lives. It helps participants notice the choices they habitually make in a more conscious manner. Everyone can try out a new role, once they see the roles that they habitually adopt.

REINFORCEMENT THROUGH THE FOUR GOLDEN POSITIONS

Scores can direct people toward particular ways to be aware of movement. The next score involves learning how to reinforce the actions we see around us. It builds on the activities of lying down, sitting, standing, and walking, which are sometimes referred to as the "Four Golden Positions" because they are the basic building blocks of all the movements we do in space.

Intention: Learn to reinforce each other's movements.
Develop spatial awareness.

SCORE

Time: 1 hour.

Space: Entire space.

People: All participants, in groups of four.

Activities:

1. Everybody gather on the periphery of the space.
2. One at a time, four people enter the space. First person: choose one of the golden positions—lying down, sitting, standing, or walking. Next person: choose a different position, being aware of its spatial relation to the first person. And so on, until all four positions are chosen.
3. Four more people enter, one at a time, each choosing one of the four positions to reinforce someone who is already there. Those already in the space do not change their positions until they have been reinforced.
4. Gradually, more and more people enter, choosing one of the four basic positions and reinforcing people who are already there.
5. When everyone is in the space, continue to develop the material, shifting from one position to another, but always with an awareness of others.

Throughout the workshop, one of our clear intents is to offer scores that allow for creative experimentation with ordinary, daily movements.

This helps non-dancers connect to the material of the dance, while increasing awareness that movements we usually think of as "pedestrian" can be a dance if we bring movement awareness to them. As a coda to the Four Golden Positions score, we take it into the Vortex Dance, encouraging participants to experiment more creatively with their movement while remaining in connection with each other and eventually forging a unity together.

SOCIAL GRAPHICS SCORE

Toward the end of the day, we do a drawing of ourselves in relation to the group. I call this "Social Graphics." It is several days into the workshop, so that people have had time to understand themselves in relation to the group.

Intention: Explore who we are as a group and how we see ourselves in relation to others.

SCORE

Time: 45 minutes.

Space: Scattered in entire space.

People: All participants, individually and in support groups.

Activities:

1. Make a drawing using dots of any colors to describe how you see yourself in relation to the whole group.
2. Share your drawing with your support group.

Who am I? Where am I? Where do I want to be? These are some of the questions to ask yourself as you do this score. Externalizing how you feel about yourself in relation to the group in a concrete image can help you make choices about your position more clearly. It provides an opportunity to make more conscious decisions and to take responsibility for how you behave in the group. People who tend to hold back may learn new ways to join in; those who take over, invading the space, may become more sensitive.

An underlying theme of this sixth day is the importance of our evolving relationships with one another and the development of a rich, shared movement language. Throughout the workshop, in the tune-ups for each day, we have been extending our movement vocabulary. Through the Active/Passive and Four Golden Positions scores we have been developing new resources for our Vortex Dance, where we move from the one to the many, coming together as a group. Allan Stinson reflects on what he has been seeing in the Vortex Dance:

Recovery

To help the group restore itself after confronting the dark side, consider the following questions:

> After an intense experience, what is the most effective way for group members to share their experiences with one another?
>
> Can noninvasive touch provide a way of communicating care and support?
>
> What scores will increase participants' awareness of different possible roles in their relations to each other?
>
> What scores will increase participants' awareness of how they are relating to each other in space?
>
> Is there a score that will lead the group to come together again in a dance of unity?
>
> Might other art forms reinforce the process? Be open to the use of visual arts, music, poetry, and song to reinforce your theme and the cohesion of your group.

While watching you dance, Anna was talking to me about the natural progression of configurations in the movement: one, twos, family groupings, tribe, nation, and so forth. And while I watched, the tribe kept coming back to me .... I thought about how in nature a group of animals really knows its own kind. Knows how it smells. Knows how it moves. Knows what it eats. Knows where it goes. Knows how to live. In the dance I saw this tribe coming to know its smell, its movement, its place, and way of being. And then I began to ask myself, what does a tribe do, what does a herd do, what does a flock do, when it senses danger? What do the reindeer do when there's something in the bush? What spirals do they form? What do the antelope do when there's a lion hiding? And I remembered that they don't take off by themselves. They don't run for their individual lives. They signal to each other. There's something they do as a group to keep the tribe alive. This is what this dance is about.

DAY 7. *Bringing the Tribe Together*

Up until this point, the daytime and evening groups have been working separately, using essentially the same scores (although more condensed for the evening group). Now we need to come together, reinforcing our sense of a single community and strengthening our trust in each other. To this end, we spend a lot of time exploring relationships and developing skills for the Vortex Dance. The Vortex Dance fosters real experiences of individual expression *and* group unity, allowing each participant to hold onto the sense of self while joining a community. We do the Vortex Dance over and over to develop our ability to be in an improvisational space with one another. Our relationship to the material deepens with this repetition.

We begin with our tune-up score, energizing our bodies with vigorous shaking movements to a strong pulse and taking this into movement throughout the space. After warming up, we bring the evening and workshop groups together by revisiting the Rising and Falling score, which is one of the central performance scores of the dance.

RISING AND FALLING REVISITED

Intention: Reexplore rising and falling as a way to evoke a personal response to the theme of life and death.

SCORE

Time: 1 hour.

Space: Entire space.

People: All participants, divided into evening and daytime groups.

Activities:

1. Daytime group: perform the Rising and Falling score while the evening group witnesses.
2. Evening group: give feedback by answering the question, "What did you see that you would like to incorporate into your performance of the score?"
3. Switch roles, with evening group performing and daytime group witnessing.

As it had before, the feedback on the Rising and Falling score brings up conflicts about making judgments. One man says, "I thought that guy was being very melodramatic. Do you want us to do that?" He keeps wanting to judge. I understand what he is talking about, but he is not following the score for feedback and his remarks come through as critical and judgmental. Two groups of people are getting together for the first time after having had different experiences working on the same material. We need for them to appreciate each other and become one group, and the only way to do that is to express appreciation and our own subjective experiences of what we have seen.

One of the things I try to do as a workshop leader is to be clear, in advance, about the score for valuacting. To many people, asking for "feedback" suggests that you are asking for criticism, so it is important to be clear about what you are looking for and to stress a focus on the positive rather than the negative. I may simply define the valuacting score this way: "As you watch people doing the Rising and Falling score, I want you to notice whether there is anything that anyone is doing that you feel you could incorporate in your movement, where you feel, 'Ahh, I wouldn't have thought of that.' The intention is not to make a judgment, but to discover new possibilities."

In this case, my score for presenting feedback is not very open. I want it to function as a way for people to support and connect with one another. I want feedback to be generative, rather than suppressive. Certainly, if someone experiences difficult emotions while witnessing, that feedback is welcome. Emotions are never judgments—they are just our experiences. But negative assessments of someone's participation in the dance are not welcome.

LEADING AND FOLLOWING

Our next score essentially repeats the Active/Passive score from the previous day. Leading and following, or finding a blend between the two, are fundamental ways of moving in relationship to other people. The possibilities derived from this exercise can be a helpful tool for participants to create relationships and a group dynamic. It gives each participant permission to take the lead, to follow, or to shift between the two roles. It encourages them to try out different choices in a nonthreatening way.

Intention: Explore leading, following, and blending with another person.

SCORE

Time: 2 hours.

Space: Scattered throughout the space.

People: All participants, in pairs (one initially passive, the other active).

Activities:

1. Sit facing your partner. Passive partner: put your palms on top of the hands of your partner then close your eyes. Active partner: keep your eyes open and, using only your hands, lead your partner into movement.

2. On the facilitator's signal, switch roles.

3. Now find a new partner. Stand in place. Passive partner: position

your hands as before and keep your eyes closed. Active partner: lead your partner in movement up, down, and to the side while keeping him or her in place. Engage the whole body. On the signal, switch roles.

4. Find yet another partner. Both partners: keep your eyes open. Alternate assuming active and passive roles, and move through space. Use your whole body. You can drop your partner's hand as the movement grows and gets more diverse.

5. Change partners again. Continue the exercise, this time with each person using different degrees of active/passive (on a scale of 1 to 10, with 1 being completely limp and 10 being totally active.)

6. With the same partner, on a signal from the facilitator, see if you can move together in a blended way, where it becomes hard to tell who is leading and who is following.

FOUR GOLDEN POSITIONS INTO VORTEX DANCE

After the Leading and Following score, we repeat the Four Golden Positions score. Both this score and the preceding one give people opportunities to lead and follow, to mirror and be mirrored. They provide movement resources as well as new experiences in relationship. These resources can be recycled into the Vortex Dance, where the kind of minute attention the participants are giving one another is essential in creating a group dance. The participants enjoy this exercise because it enables them to quickly become an ensemble of movers.

Intention: Work with the Four Golden Positions.
                Generate movement resources for the Vortex Dance.

SCORE

Time: 1 hour.

Space: Scattered throughout the room.

People: All participants, in two groups.

Activities:

1. Divide into two groups.
2. Group 1: enter the space one by one and choose whether to lie down, sit, stand, or walk.
3. After everyone in Group 1 has entered, Group 2 enter one by one, each person reinforcing someone from Group 1.
4. Building on these elements, begin the Vortex Dance.

We perform this score twice. Each time the group divides into two, they divide in new ways. The score enables people to make many new relationship choices. One participant comments, "I was initially attracted to someone walking quite slowly in a single line. When I reinforced his walk, we fell into a calm eye in the storm around us. As we continued to walk together, simple but profound changes in our movement seemed to create new relationships between us and ourselves, as a unit, and within the group. We might turn opposite from one another as we reached our limit in space or turn into ourselves. Each case contained a microcosm of experience. We began vocalizing together; each sound was like a call. Others joined us and contributed new changes in movement and relationship. New sounds emerged. The whole thing generated a powerful sense of 'here are some rules' and 'here you can create organic change and affect the group.' Eventually I felt the larger dance begin to take on our power. Tempo and feeling were transmitted somehow. From the eye to the storm, a sense of order with diversity was created. It seemed to me that this experience embodied the true nature of collective unity experienced through independent movement."

BUILDING A MOUNTAIN

The Vortex Dance is a metaphor for group connectivity. First you connect to yourself and then you connect to another person. You don't just go from A to Z; there are all these steps in between. It's an evolutionary process. Within our differences we are searching for a common pulse. Once we've reached this consensus, a common beat in the sound of our feet on the ground, we build upon the group spirit it expresses. We move from dancing alone to dancing in duets and trios. We build human families, finding our community and then our tribe. Finally we join as a whole in the center and build a symbol of our strength. We've gotten together, forming a big, strong group, but now we need to reach out and connect with a greater life force. Moving upward suggests a searching and yearning for that great force beyond—a reaching beyond our limits, beyond our comfortable boundaries.

Intention: Create a climax to the Vortex Dance.
SCORE
Time: 30 minutes.
Space: Centered in the space.
People: All participants.
Activities:
1. Facilitator: choose a few people to be lifted in the air.
2. Gather in the center and practice lifting them as a unit, making sure that they are protected in the back and the front.

Building a
mountain.
© Jay Graham
Photographer. Anna
Halprin Papers;
courtesy of Museum
of Performance
and Design,
San Francisco.

This moment of lifting people up can be very exuberant, but it can also feel precarious. To make sure that a sense of safety is maintained along with the exuberance, the score has to be closed in some ways, with particular roles assigned. Coming as it does after the extremely open Vortex score, where people are free to choose their own activities and relationships, the shift may stir up emotions. I choose the people to be lifted with practicality in mind—each is light and has extensive movement experience.

To reinforce the experience of moving upward, we do a bird visualization. Everyone draws an image of a special bird—a messenger that can soar high above, flying far, to carry a vision of health and peace to the planet.

ADDITIONAL MOVEMENT RESOURCES

Before we move into rehearsing for the performance, I introduce additional scores to develop more movement resources. In particular, these scores are intended to generate resources for the final score in the performance, the Sound Spiral.

UPPER SPINE MOBILIZATION

Intention: Increase range of movement in upper spine.

SCORE

Time: 30 minutes.

Space: Entire space.

People: All participants, in partners.

Activities:

1. Sit back-to-back and breathe together, feeling your partner's breath and the contours of each other's backs.
2. One person bend forward. Other person: lean backward onto your partner's back. Change the position of your arms (down, side, or overhead) to modulate the range of extension and hyperextension in your upper spine. If you feel any strain in your back or neck, slide your pelvis forward, away from your partner's back.
3. Slowly move back to "center," sitting back-to-back.
4. Alternate roles.
5. Add breathing sounds.

SWINGING INTO SPACE

Intention: Coordinate arm movement with movement into space.

SCORE

Time: 30 minutes.

Space: Entire space.

People: All participants.

Activities:

1. Stand and swing one arm forward and backward while holding the shoulder with the other hand to feel the in-and-out rotation of the shoulder joint.
2. Follow the movement with your eyes.
3. Repeat on the other side.
4. Follow through with a forward-and-back swing. Allow the momentum of the swing to take the movement into space.

SHIFTING TO PERFORMANCE REHEARSAL

Toward the end of a long day, we are ready to do a run-through of the performance. The ritual or performative act is different from the workshop process, and at this point in the workshop I, as the group leader, make choices about how to present our story to the witnesses. Many of the scores used in the performance are closed, created by me and my collaborators, and presented to the group as part of the performance ritual. These are performance scores. In the workshop, we learn them while continuing to do more open scores that generate community, movement resources, and personal experience.

There is resistance on the part of the group to this shift from workshop to performance mode; after spending so many days together involved in a deep and personal process, it is difficult for the participants to relinquish some of their free will and follow the closed scores I have created. But I do this for many reasons. The most important is my belief that the work we do must be shared with a group of witnesses in order to focalize and empower our intent; in order for that act to have power, it must be shaped in specific ways. What I have learned about the creation of dances and rituals has taken a lifetime of study; at this point in the workshop process, I begin to guide the group toward the creation of an effective ritual. It is my hope that we will create a dance that will serve the greater intent of the ritual, for the group members as well as the witnesses who attend the performance.

The scores for the performance are arranged to follow the Five Stages of Healing: identification, confrontation, release and restoration, change, and assimilation. This mirrors the structure of our workshop days, where we have spent a lot of time identifying the dance's life-and-death theme, confronting our demons, releasing them, restoring ourselves, and moving toward change.

We begin with identification, presenting our central theme—life and death—with the Rising and Falling score and stating our intention with "I Want to Live!" Before we move on to the next stage—confronting illness and death—we prepare ourselves to face the fears associated with the dark side. We do this by doing the Vortex Dance together, finding our power and strength as a community rather than remaining in isolation. The group needs all the strength, power, and affirmation it can mobilize before taking on the arduous task of facing and confronting its demons. We have to become a collective body dancing in community.

In the confrontation section, we develop the Monster (Mask) and Warrior scores, with a special role assigned to the audience (see day 9). Stomping rhythmically on the ground, lines of Warriors urge the Monsters to emerge from the group. The Monsters become living masks, distorting their faces in disgusting ways, which takes a lot of courage to do in public and inevitably brings up awful feelings. Only those who are facing a life-threatening illness are asked to do the Monster Dance in the performance (although if they don't feel up to it, they can choose someone to do it for them). The other participants give support as the Warriors. The dance is the confrontation; enacting it provides release.

After the powerful experience of the Warrior Dance and the catharsis that comes from confronting the dark side, the Monster dancers are ready to make peace with their circumstances and begin to re-create relationships with others in the human community. This is the moment in the healing process where a recognition of suffering as a human experience can be made, and where compassion and deeper relationships can be fostered. This is a delicate and intimate time, and we take a variety of actions to support and develop this atmosphere. It is important to find a safe place where we can rest after the intensity of the confrontation dance. The Warriors become caregivers, holding, rocking, and soothing those who have just confronted their demons. There are moments of quiet tenderness between dancers as the group takes time to reconnect with their inner strengths as well as the supportive container of the group. Everybody joins in to sing the song "Restore Me" (see day 9).

THE BRIDGE

As we move from release and restoration to the stage of change, a transition is needed. This is a moment when the emotional state of the dance and the content of the dance changes. We are beginning to resolve our own personal issues of grief and loss, connect to the larger grief and loss of the collective body, and are ready to move toward experiences of change and faith. This score was designed for the performance, intended as a transition from the Restoration into the Earth Run, which is the next score in the performance.

Intention: Transition from one healing state to another.
SCORE
Time: 20 minutes or more.
Space: Entire space.
People: All participants.
Activities:
1. Form two concentric half-circles with partners from the Restoration score facing each other, one sitting and one standing.
2. Standing partner: assist sitting partner to a standing position.
3. Form a bridge with your partner.
4. After all the pairs have formed a bridge, begin a procession, with

the last couple in line walking under the entire arc of participants, looking at and connecting with others in the bridge, then the next pair of dancers in line walking through the bridge, and so on. (If your partner is unable to stand up by him- or herself, get someone to help carry your partner and proceed through the bridge.)

5. As you come out of the bridge, join the line the first couple has started and form a large circle around the periphery of the space.

Once everyone has passed through the bridge and joined the large circle, the participants kneel in preparation for the Earth Run, which is intended to mobilize change. The dancers are now dancing not only for themselves, but also for each other and for all life on the planet. This is the same intention as when we do the Earth Run on the mountain.

SOUND SPIRAL

After the Earth Run, we integrate what we have done and learned with the Sound Spiral, making a link from the dancers to the audience (our witnesses). This score expands our community to include the witnesses. It also serves as a symbolic way of placing ourselves in relationship to that which exists beyond us in the larger world. It represents the beginning of growth and integration, a shift from a view that only includes the individual to a view that encompasses community, the social order, and a larger global reality. The Sound Spiral is the final performance score of *Circle the Earth*.

Intention: Expand our community.
SCORE
Time: 5 minutes.
Space: Entire space.
People: All participants.
Activities:

1. One person: stand in the center of the room, make a resonating sound, then spin in a counterclockwise direction.
2. Another person: join in, also moving counterclockwise and adding to the sound.
3. A third, then a fourth person join, and so on, with more and more people joining the circle and adding their sounds.
4. Continue spiraling toward the outer edge of the room. Increase your speed and move in unison.
5. Extend your arms into space horizontally as you begin to run.

Score by Terry Riley
as possible warm-
up for Sound Spiral.
Image © Terry Riley.

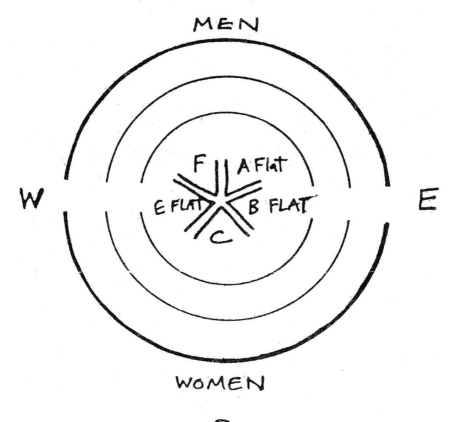

N

MEN

W

E

F · A Flat
E FLAT · B FLAT
C

WOMEN

S

a) Inner pie-shape circle
   slowly turn
b) Arms up and extended
c) Sing your note to people
   in outer circle
d) Use intervals of silence
e) Outer Three circles sing
The note passed to you by
pie-shaped circle.
RESULT → Five notes swirl around
                   circle

Bringing the Tribes Together

As the emphasis shifts from a workshop toward a public performance, consider these questions:

How can you facilitate the transition from workshop to performance?

What is the intention of the performance, and how do the scores you have done earlier in the week support this?

Is everyone comfortable with the performance scores? If not, what issues still need to be addressed?

What will motivate your group to engage with the opportunity to perform?

Is your leadership team in good communication with the participants and attentive to any potential uneasiness about the performance?

6. Run smoothly, lightly, and in unison. Cover more and more floor space.
7. When the group reaches the periphery of the room, everyone turn and face the witnesses.
8. Place your hands on your hearts. Bend your knees and rise up, releasing your arms upward. Then, as you breathe out, make a "Pah" sound.

At the conclusion of the performance, the witnesses will be invited to join the dancers in a celebratory Victory Dance.

DAY 8. *Moving into Performance*

After the previous night's run-through, a group of us create a graphic representation of the score for the entire dance on butcher paper. At the start of the day everybody gathers around this score, looking at it and studying it silently. I go through each panel of the score, reviewing the dance. People are encouraged to write down any questions and share them later in their support groups. This viewing and reviewing afford an opportunity to look at the whole piece at once, observing how parts are connected and noticing how the space is used. It gives participants a chance to voice concerns about what isn't clear or seems unresolved, as well as to identify places where more transition seems needed.

Before we walk through all the scores, in preparation for our dress rehearsal that night, we have a group meeting to strongly direct everyone toward performance and make it clear that this is not an ordinary performance but a ritual. The performers need to understand their roles in a different way—not as stars or supporters, foreground or background—and to get beyond their egos or any issues of specialness. It is crucial that they listen not only to their own needs but also to the needs of the group and the needs of the ritual. To find that balance, the performers must get in touch with their original intention in coming here—whether to confront AIDS or to support those challenging AIDS—and to get totally behind that intention. A ritual is an act of creative human magic, and our intention is the portal into the altered reality of the ritual. Anything that distracts—our petty feelings about not being the star, our sense of incompleteness or smallness—saps power from the dance.

DRESS REHEARSAL

Leading up to the dress rehearsal, the day is less about participating in a workshop than about moving into a different attitude. It is about preparing to become performers, finding the meaning for and understanding the role of each person in the ritual. None of us really knows what it will be like to perform with witnesses, but there is an expectancy in the space and a quiet concentration.

A small group of witnesses are invited to see the dress rehearsal. For the most part they are people who have been involved in earlier creations of *Circle the Earth*, people who understand the process and can give useful feedback. The dress rehearsal goes very well, much to everyone's relief. Now we know that we can do it. Still, there are parts that seem mechanically awkward, and others that seem to lack "juice." How to resolve this?

One score that seems to beg for reworking is the ending. Instead of waiting around passively for me to solve the problem, self-appointed leaders start calling out suggestions. Although none of these suggestions fully works for me, the different participants' ideas become valuable resources and lead me to design a closing score, the Victory Dance (see day 9), which joins the performers to the witnesses and engages everyone. In the score that evolves, the witnesses are invited to join the performers in a joyful yet deliberate procession through a series of arches made by the performers that ends in a series of connecting circles that accommodate everyone.

Collective creativity is tricky. Just how do decisions get made? How does each person participate and to what extent? In this piece I try to make it clear from the beginning where the decision-making and final responsibility will lie—that is my role. Not everybody, however, understands my role so clearly. Adhering to the ideal and practice of collective creativity is particularly tricky in a large group of people working under a performance deadline. During the workshop, especially in the beginning days, each person is given the opportunity to discover how he or she might connect the collective scores to his or her own life. Time is devoted to open discussion and other exercises so that participants can generate as many resources for themselves and the dance as possible. But there comes a point where the process must shift. Input and resources have to be focused on the task at hand. This change is not always welcomed or understood well by the whole group.

This business about "roles" is one of the most difficult and challenging issues in creating group rituals. In a traditional ritual, it is clear which community members hold which roles. The rabbi, the priestess, and the shaman all have their jobs in the context of the ritual; the participants—the community members—also have their specific tasks. One of the things we have lost in modern culture is the knowledge of our place in the context of ritual, and because so many of the traditional rituals have been emptied of meaning for us, we are often adrift in understanding how to prepare ourselves to participate in a ritual enactment. So we get caught up in questions like: What is my role? How can I participate? What is allowed? What does it mean to be a "leader"? Who decides? Who chooses? Questions of authority, specialness, honor, visibility, equality, difference, commonality, individuality, and group are troublesome, but they arise from fertile ground. The underlying question is: How can we feel both fully ourselves and yet also completely connected to one another?

One participant in the Warrior Dance feels "pushed around by people who didn't participate in the process with us and then were set in front of us as leaders, as if the group itself didn't have the resources to develop these qualities." (These "leaders" are "ancestors of the dance," people who have done *Circle the Earth* many times before and have come to give their support.) This person's words are important. There is a way in which we are all being "pushed around" by forces, being led by something we cannot quite see as ourselves, not yet claim as our own. Ritual time and space have their own shape and power. If we can each find our own place within this time and space, the place where our own deepest expression and that of the collective join, then perhaps our awareness will shift. We will see that what pushes us around can propel us and that those who guide us are not leading because they are in front of us, but because they are behind us one hundred percent. This is the kind of shift in consciousness needed for the ritual to be healing.

DAY 9. *Performance Day*

As the performance time approaches, I keep going over the feedback from the witnesses at the dress rehearsal. The transition to the Vortex Dance still seems problematic to me. Something vital seems missing. Somehow we aren't going deep enough, we're not getting at the heart of it. So I come up with a game called "Tell the Truth," which we try out the morning of the performance.

TELL THE TRUTH

My score is intended to deal with questions of collective decision-making. It is a good example of how personal issues can get turned into art experiences and how that process in itself can help resolve problems. It is also an example of how a group can confront the issues within the dance they are creating. This score will affect *how* we do the dance, but it does not become a score in the performance itself. It is more valuable as a way of clarifying the context in which we dance and the relationships between dancers.

Intention: Make visible the performers' real-life connections with each other.

SCORE

Time: As long as necessary.

Space: In front of where the witnesses will be.

People: All participants.

Activities:

1. Sit facing the imaginary witnesses.
2. One HIV-positive person: stand up and call out the name of your support person.
3. Support person: stand up.
4. HIV-positive person: tell the support person why you have chosen him or her.
5. Support person: respond verbally and/or nonverbally.

When we first do the score, the HIV-positive participant is asked to call out his or her support person, but not to reveal the reasons why. Steps 4 and 5 are added in a recycling of the score, as I feel something is missing. It is clear to me that the content of our relationships isn't being revealed. Although I question the wisdom of opening up this issue so close to the performance itself, I decide to take the risk. The next time we do the score, I ask each person *why* she or he chose to call on this particular friend for support. People in the group are encouraged to speak about their love, but also about their prejudices, fear of death, and sense of isolation. At first people can't tap into their emotions. I keep pressing for the truth. Finally, one woman asks her caregiver, "Are you still afraid of getting AIDS from me?" Her caregiver responds, "No, now I'm afraid of not living my life fully." The vulnerability and honesty that eventually come out are so touching it is almost unbearable.

A young man tells us that he cannot grieve enough because so many of his friends are gone. He recites a long litany of death and dying. "I look around and ask myself—who is next? Are you next, are you next, am I next?" (Sadly, he would die shortly after the performance.)

One female caregiver says to her partner, "I think my teenage son is gay. I've grown to love and respect you so much that I've decided to bring him from our home in Colorado to this performance so he can meet you." (Five years later I learn her son has died of AIDS.)

Emotions run high. There is crying and hugging and everyone in the group is reminded of why they are dancing this dance. This is our missing link. The experience provides us with a different kind of performance skill, the power of being honest and open and totally present before witnesses. When people are really expressing the truth of what is going on between them, we all know it. Those moments are very compelling; they sweep through the whole group.

This "little game" becomes part of the group's self-portrait. It shows that we have come to speak a common language and have developed enough trust to say honestly and clearly who we are, what we believe, and what we want from one another. "Tell the Truth" directly confronts the central issues of the dance: the circle of prejudice, isolation, fear, and death surrounding people with HIV, and the need for a new circle of trust, care, and life. Many difficult truths are spoken, and people reconnect both to the personal nature of the dance and to why they are there as participants.

Although I help shape this score, it is not something that comes fully formed from my head; rather, it evolves from the resources the group provides, from their own experiences, prejudices, longings, and love. This is an important lesson about this kind of ritual-making: we can't think our way to an end result; instead, we set up scores that generate resources, which create the path that we walk together. The only way these honest and pertinent scores can arise is from the specificity of the group doing the ritual. Any dance made about any meaningful issue will have many of these poignant moments of connection that can be used in the creation of a final performative ritual. The group members become more committed to one another as their personal myths grow, while the collective myth of the dance takes on more life in the form of the real stories of real people and their desire to live together and care for one another.

DESIGNING THE SET FOR THE PERFORMANCE

Creating a meaningful ritual involves preparations for both the performers and the performance space. For *Circle the Earth: Dancing with Life on the Line*, our task is to turn a cavernous high-school gymnasium into a site for a meaningful ritual. This is quite a stretch! We are lucky to have Joseph Stubblefield as our set designer, and he involves the entire group in the creation of our set from the beginning of the workshop. Just as we use movement scores that allow people's participation to shape the dance, he creates a score for designing the space that entails group participation.

At the end of the first day of the workshop, each participant was asked to bring a rock "the size of your skull" to the gymnasium. Over the course of the week these rocks were used in the creation of the set. It is important for the performers to contribute to the creation of the environment in which they will dance, and also important that their contributions include objects that have personal meaning. A personal object can function as a container for the emotions, fantasies, insights, dreams, and associations generated during the workshop. The rock serves as a special place for a dancer to meditate or "talk" about questions and insights that arise. Because the rocks become part of the set, the performers can then bring this information with them into the performance itself. In addition, the act of bringing in an object from outside the performance space connects the ritual to the larger world, and can in turn help bring some of the energy generated in the ritual back into the world when the performance is finished.

Although the initial idea to use the rocks comes from the designer, the evolution of the set is a collaborative process, with input from the performers throughout the workshop process. For the performance, the rocks hang from long cords attached to the ceiling in the back of the space, forming a square. This environment makes a strong emotional and visual statement. People give it different names: the rain forest, the garden, the prayer space, the meditation space, the memorial.

The power of the rocks' symbolism comes out in a story told later by one of the performers: "I went to my friend's house, and his roommate was in the process of landscaping. They were building a little retainer wall and I thought to take a rock from there because his roommate is posi-

Stage set for *Circle the Earth: Dancing with Life on the Line.* © Jay Graham Photographer. Anna Halprin Papers; courtesy of Museum of Performance and Design, San Francisco.

tive, and my friend has AIDS. I brought the rock in, even though I didn't have a clue as to what the rock was about. But I painted it and hung it up. And then right before the performance, I got it. It has been sitting there all week absorbing all of our energy. I just sat with it for a while right at my heart level. I could feel this solid, energetic force, encompassing all of what we had been doing all week.

"I took it back to my friend's house a couple of weeks later. He hadn't been able to make it to the performance because he was ill. I told him where the rock had gone, where it had come from, where it had journeyed, and I left it on his front porch. A couple of days later, it was gone. Then yesterday, after my friend died, we were tearing his place apart, and I found it right under the bed, right under where his heart had been for his last weeks. When I saw him last, he said to me, 'Thank you for your strength,' but I didn't get it. As I was walking to the car, I saw in my mind's eye that rock under his bed. I know that he got a lot out of it, because of what we put into it."

When I think about the dancers and how they were able to imbue the simplest of objects with meaning, I see how dances like *Circle the Earth* can create an opportunity to make sense out of the struggles and challenges of our lives. We live in a world that has almost been emptied of the sacred; in *Circle the Earth* we learn how to reinvest everything—our movements, our gestures, our relationships, the rocks around us—with sacred meaning.

In addition to the rocks, our set includes four altars that we create in each of the four directions, bringing our experience outdoors on the mountain into the indoor performance space. The dancers bring fruit and flowers to decorate these altars. The lavish and beautiful series of altars will stand during the performance and be dismantled at its end. Not only do these altars transform the place where we perform from a mundane space into a sacred one, but they also provide an echo of our theme of life and death, offering nourishment before disappearing.

PREPARING THE DANCERS FOR PERFORMANCE

Before we perform, we provide a formal time for preparation. This preparatory time cultivates a heightened awareness of the healing aspects of the dance for all of us. After adorning the four direction altars, the dancers visit each one, stopping at the direction that holds special significance for them. These meditative visits to the altars help the participants remember why they are doing the dance.

In the space we also hang a score of the entire dance, which graphically illustrates all the activities of the performance, so everyone can see the evolving floor pattern and where they fit into it. This gives us a larger view of the dance and an opportunity to look at it from a more artistic and objective standpoint. We can see how all the parts of the dance follow sequentially, and the nature of the transitions becomes clear. This is also an opportunity to appreciate ourselves as parts of a whole that makes this dance possible. The dancers are encouraged to remain quiet and thoughtful as they study this score and ready themselves for the performance.

A highlight of the preparation period occurs when spiritual and community leaders give their blessings to the performers. A Jewish rabbi, a Zen Buddhist monk, a Shinto priest, a Native American healer, an African American Baptist minister, and a Unitarian minister grace us with their understanding of the power of the dance. Some pray, some chant, some read poetry, and all bless the dancers. We have been through our personal experiences in the workshop and are now calling on the larger collective body of witnesses to help us do this dance not only for ourselves, but also for everyone. We are dancing our prayers, and these spiritual leaders acknowledge this. The blessings from different traditions remind us of our common search for the sacred, as well as the diverse traditions that support us. "Dance the dance with a passion for life that emerges from the depth of suffering," the Reverend Sandy Winter calls out. "Remember that you belong to the universe and *dance the dance*."

The workshop is like an inhalation; the performance is like an exhalation; the preparation is the space between the breaths. The dancers take time to get comfortable in the performance space, appreciating the environment and doing whatever activities they feel will prepare them for the performance itself. As one participant later describes it: "The hour before the performance was a vision of paradise for me. We saw the feathers purified with sage smoke, heard from religious leaders, and got to roam around to the altars and the rocks, stretching, meditating, centering—just being in the space. That was one of the most sacred times for me."

PREPARING THE WITNESSES

Before the event begins, while the dancers are still going through their preparations, the witnesses are led to a different space for their own initiation into *Circle the Earth*. I greet them and offer some thoughts to prepare them for the performance. I speak to them about the development of the dance through the workshop process, our intention in doing this dance ritual, and our desire for their participation. They are briefed on the nature of their role—to support the performers in their dance and to allow themselves to be moved and changed. They are advised about the masks sitting on their seats for the Monster Dance, and they are told why and when and how to wear them.

The witnesses are also told that there will be a pathway of light to lead them from their gathering place into the performance space. Each performer has prepared a luminary (a bag with a candle inside) and placed it along the path. Each candle is lit in someone's memory, creating a link not only between witnesses and performers, but also between the living and the dead. Our dance is a call for help for the living, as well as an honoring of those who have died. The pathway offers the witnesses an opportunity to transition from the secular to the sacred realm as they enter the gymnasium where the dance will take place. The witnesses are encouraged to use the time before the performance to meditate on what in themselves they want healed and for whom they wish to pray. Musicians initiate the procession of the witnesses into the space; the evocative sound of their bagpipes and drums moves us all.

When I first greet the witnesses, I emphasize: "Everything you will witness tonight is real." An avalanche of emotions that I have been storing up comes roaring out. More than anything I want to convey that the performance can be a healing for all of us. We are not trying to entertain an audience. We are not really doing this dance for them. And yet we need them so that we can make the dance real for us. I ask the witnesses to be as real and as full and as honest in their responses as the performers are in their own.

Performing dance as a ritual does not mean that it lacks aesthetic qualities. The ritual may be enhanced if its outward form is beautiful. But the criterion for whether the ritual is successful is not whether it pleases, in some aesthetic way, the people who come to view it, but whether the dance has accomplished its purpose. That's why we don't call the people who come to our performances "the audience." They need to embody and understand their role in a different way, so we call them "witnesses."

I learned about the power of the witnesses through a Native American ceremony. In 1989 I saw the Sun Dance, a sacred Native American dance that requires great fortitude and courage on the part of the dancers. The dance was held in Davis, California, at the D-Q University for Native Americans in honor of one of their leaders who had been incarcerated. People's emotions were running high. My husband and I were the only non-Indians attending, and we were doing everything we could to fit in and show our respect.

This dance involves piercing of the skin. Bear claws are inserted into the chest and attached to leather thongs, which are in turn attached to a tree in the center of the dance space. In a trance state, the dancers move around this tree and when they feel ready, face the tree and begin to pull away from it until the bear claws rip through their skin. One dancer was having trouble as the claws would not release him. Blood was streaming down his chest while he continued in greater and greater determination to break through. A leader of the dance stood behind him and added his weight to the dancer's pull in an effort to help him. A group of women lined up behind him and began to chant. The witnesses sitting or standing in a circle around the dance area were motionless, eyes straight ahead in silent concentration. The atmosphere was tense. My husband was empathizing so strongly with the dancer's struggle and pain that he turned pale and became so weak he seemed about to faint. As I turned to look in his direction, an old woman sitting next to me instantly picked up a twig and gave me a crashing wallop across my shins. I knew instinctively what

The Five Stages of Healing and *Circle the Earth*

Circle the Earth uses the Five Stages of Healing as a template for the performance scores. The scores are ordered in accord with the first four stages of healing, following a proven trajectory for personal and social transformation. The last stage — Assimilation — is what follows the performance.

Identification
    "I Want to Live!"
    Rising and Falling
    Vortex Dance
Confrontation
    Monster/Mask Dance
    Warrior Dance
Restoration
    Restore Me
    Bridge
Change
    Earth Run
    Sound Spiral
    Victory Dance

she was saying: "You are here to pray for the dancer. Don't forget for an instant. Pay attention."

Our dance is not as intense or culturally storied as the Sun Dance, but for us it is deeply meaningful and likewise needs the committed attention of its witnesses for its success. I make sure those who come to see *Dancing with Life on the Line* understand their role as witnesses before they enter the performance space, that they are committed to this kind of devoted attention.

AND WE BEGIN . . .

When the witnesses are ready, a signal is sent to the gymnasium. The performers line up in two long rows on either side to await the witnesses. As the bagpipes play, the witnesses are led down the candlelit path into the gym. As they stream into the gym, I look and see what *they* must be taking in — the performers in the carefully designed environment. It is as if I am seeing Joseph Stubblefield's environmental design and the ways the colors of the performers' costumes link together for the first time.

Bodies of blues and reds and yellows and purples stretch from one end of the gym to the other, magnifying the vastness of the space, taking the eye back to a powerful black-and-white-striped banner hanging from the ceiling, and beneath it one hundred rocks suspended four feet from the floor on black-and-white ropes, shimmering in the light. All are symbols for me of life and death, the theme of the dance. It hits me all of a sudden that Joseph, out of his own confrontation with cancer, has created an environment that is as rich and powerful in images as Allan Stinson's words are in giving voice to the dance.

FEATHER RUNNING

We begin our ritual with the feather running ceremony that we first connected with before our day on the mountain (see "A Special Ceremony" on day 1). The feather running ceremony brings symbols from outside the gymnasium into the sacred space of the dance. The feathers symbolize the history of *Circle the Earth*, the ancestors of this dance, and the efficacy of the dance for our whole community. Beginning on a ceremonial note situates our dance in the realm of ritual—the calling in of the ancestors, the calling on the power of the natural world, and the commitment to our fierce intention all frame the ritual that follows.

IDENTIFICATION

"I Want to Live!"

The performers form a pathway for a run by those living with HIV or AIDS, making them visible. Each runner calls out: "My name is _____ and I WANT TO LIVE," running or walking down the pathway with conviction. This score is saying to the audience: We want you, as our witnesses, to be in alignment with what this dance is about. We want you to know that we are dancing for our lives. And we want you to know that this is real. That *we want to live.*

When you experience that declaration as a witness it can be extremely unsettling. There is no way you can hear that call for life, and witness the person running, and not realize that each of these performers is living with the sentence of HIV and is out there dancing for his or her life. One witness says, "I couldn't even look at people when they were coming down saying 'I want to live.' I felt like they were saying 'I'm going to die,' even though they weren't. It was very confrontive and very real." Even though the score is incredibly dramatic, that is not its purpose; it is designed to put the performers and the witnesses into a mutual alignment with our struggle for life.

"'I Want to Live' was the start of a commitment to this process," one

Performance of
"I Want to Live!"
Photo: Coni Beeson.

of the performers later recalls. "It was a bit frightening for me. I have a lot of issues around vulnerability and adequacy. And I had my friends up there. The strangers really didn't matter to me. Coming forward and declaring my desire for life changed my attitude about being public with my illness. Before that I had been shy and concerned about being asked publicly, but after *Circle the Earth*, I'm not at all concerned about being public with it. I couldn't say I am *proud* (because who is proud to have a life-threatening illness?), but I am proud to be part of a community that takes such a strong stand on the side of life."

Another performer says, "When everyone did that it felt so full of life. Because at that moment, for the five minutes of the score, everyone was affirming their own lives and that they wanted to live."

Rising and Falling
"The dance begins as life begins," Allan Stinson states. As he will do at different times during the performance, he speaks directly to the witnesses in prose and verse, offering a narrative for the score. His words draw on the workshop experience and what different participants have expressed.

When you perform an identifying score like Rising and Falling with your community, is there a poem that speaks to the specific issue you are facing?

WE ARE THE BREATH OF THE EARTH.
Her inspiration and her expiration
Flow through us.
We are the breath of the Earth
Out of the Earth for a moment
Then into her arms again.
From the first breath to last sigh
We are Earth and we are Earth.
We are here and we are gone . . . .

The dancers rise and fall, just as the breath rises and falls. No value is expressed in this rhythm. It is the cycle of life and death, expansion and contraction. The movement is neutral and indifferent to moral evaluations. Although we may form many associations, no value statement is made in this section of the dance. We are simply showing a natural pattern, the rhythm of being.

This dance offers the performers a chance to get in touch with where they are in terms of their commitment to both life and death. To rise from lying down to standing is like going from birth to life; later you may fall down again, dying and returning to earth. In that process you make the transition from one world of reality to another world of reality. You transform yourself by tapping into the deepest levels of your being. And when you decide to stand or decide to lie down, it's as if you've gotten in touch at the deepest level with who you are, where you are at that particular moment, before you start the dance.

"I confronted my own death," one of the dancers reports. "When I fell it was real. And then to be reborn and to die and to be reborn and to die again and again. When I live with the fact of my death, every moment is more important and I value my life more. I don't have time to fool around and waste my life on inconsequential matters." Another performer echoes these words: "I got in touch with the feeling of living and then dying. I remember this kind of pluck or twang from the musicians, and to me it was like the cord of life snapping. And at that point, that was my death. I fell to the ground. Then I got to rise again, to experience a kind of rebirth."

Vortex Dance

We have spent a lot of time in the workshop gathering resources for the Vortex Dance. In some ways, this dance has been a community laboratory where we have explored the connection of the one to the many, how to maintain fidelity to our own movements while committing ourselves to the movement of the collective. The more we do this dance, the less outside direction is needed. Often, a simple directive like "Walk until you find a common pulse" is enough to start the process. And this is a dance that is never done the same way twice—its open score encourages new explorations every time we do it. In performance, we frame the dance with a spoken-word piece narrated by Allan Stinson, connecting us to the dance of all the living beings around us.

> The One reveals itself as many
> And the many find themselves to be One.
> Within Life there are many tribes.
> Yet each tribe is one and knows its own kind.
>
> The redwoods stand together.
> The dolphins play together.
> The flocks of geese fly north with a single soul.
> Even the bear, which loves to live alone,
> Must find and dance with bear
> For the bear tribe to go on.
>
> But what of the tribe of people—
> We who set ourselves apart from other tribes
> And sometimes from each other?
> How do we come to know our own kind?
> How do we gather together?

The shaping and forming of community in the Vortex Dance happen nonverbally and consensually through movement. Within the larger collective configuration, there are small individual dances of surprising diversity. One person is lifted into the air; others run and jump onto one another and fall to the ground, again and again; yet another cluster crawls slowly along the floor. Somewhere, a group starts to chant, while another begins to sway and is gradually reinforced by others until a procession, which attracts more and more people, begins. Although these diverse activities may appear random and even chaotic, there is a selective process going on. The energy of the group gives rise to a liberation in each of us that is difficult to find when dancing alone. Others then mirror this freedom back to us. A larger power, a deep collective physical intelligence, directs the choreography.

Watching the Vortex Dance during the performance, I think of a Brueghel painting of a country fair in a small village. In the painting, a series of unrelated things happen simultaneously. It is hard for the eye to find a single focus. Yet, despite the apparent chaos in the painting, there are elements that connect the diversity of the village scene, much as they do in the Vortex Dance. Acceptance of difference and diversity within a field of what is common ultimately brings the performers to a unifying closure, where we build a mountain of people in the center of the space. This dance can feel spontaneous and fun for the performers, but in many ways it requires a lot from the viewers. The witnesses are given a chance to observe the ways in which a group goes from an individual to a community, but to perceive this, they must be willing to suspend all judgments about what dance should be—that is what will allow them to see something totally new.

One of our dancers later says, "The dance that comes to me when I think about *Circle the Earth* as a performance is the Vortex Dance. It is so powerful, almost as if I left my body and can see it from the outside. Because even though I was participating, I have a picture of what that looked like. I see this great swirl of people moving powerfully. And I imagine that it all looks something like the photographs we see in pictures of the universe where there are a lot of stars or planets that might be very far apart. A galaxy of people, spinning around independently yet in one great unit. So I think the Vortex Dance expresses independence and unity at the same time."

CONFRONTATION

At the end of the Vortex Dance everybody descends to the floor in a cluster. The narrator comes in and warns the community that it is threatened, that a danger is lurking. "And when there is danger present / A healthy tribe takes care of each other," he reminds them.

As the specter of AIDS is alluded to, the dancers begin to form a line that will be the starting point for the Warrior and Monster Dances. It's the performative equivalent of the dancers drawing their line in the sand and saying, "Enough is enough!"

> OUT! OUT! OUT! OUT!
> We're drawing the line.
> Our lives are on the line.
> OUT! OUT! OUT! OUT!...

The dancers move in a confrontational line toward the witnesses, who feel viscerally the performers' embodied experiences of living with their lives on the line. This is a particularly intense part of the dance, where performers and witnesses are united in their shared desire for healing and for life.

The Warrior and Monster Dances

The confrontation consists of two separate scores performed by two groups of dancers, the Warriors and the Monsters, plus a third score performed by the witnesses (the audience). Those with life-threatening illnesses do the Monster Dance, while everyone else performs the Warrior Dance.

The Warriors, with their large, firm movements, are powerful, both spiritually and physically. They take on the responsibility of backing up those doing the Monster Dance, giving them strength and energy. As one Warrior dancer expresses it, "My intention is to give my power to the people who are fighting for their lives. I support them with all my energy, and all my being." And a Monster dancer says, "I don't think I could have embodied my Monster without hearing the Warriors behind me."

This is the performance score for the Warriors:

1. Form lines according to the color of your costume. Link arms.
2. Move forward in unison for a distance of 10 to 20 feet. Do the Warrior movement (see day 4).
3. Move backward, while facing downstage for a distance of 10 to 20 feet.
4. Repeat steps 2 and 3.

The Monsters gather behind the Warriors. They do not directly use the masks that they drew in the workshop, although they hold those powerful and visually dramatic images in mind. Instead, the Monsters distort their faces to embody the dark and destructive side, presenting those "masks" to the witnesses. By using their actual faces, the performers are more successful in *becoming* the Monster. They revive the kinesthetic sensations from which the mask images were drawn and trigger the emotions necessary to confront the dark side.

This is the performance score for the Monster Dance:

1. Assume the facial mask you drew in the workshop and maintain a focus on your face.
2. Guided by the spirit of your mask, and with the highest level of

Performance of
Monster Dance.
Photographer
unknown.

intensity, come downstage and make your way through the lines of
Warriors toward the witnesses.

3. Allow your Monster to move and speak through you.
4. Pace your movement so that by the time you have reached the line
   of witnesses, you will be exhausted.
5. Collapse on the floor.

The Monsters must break through the flanks of Warriors as they hurl
themselves forward. This intensifies their struggle as they press through
that wall to the other side, where the witnesses form another sort of wall,
hemming the Monsters in.

The Witnesses' Score

Each Monster performer has a different dance, uniquely tied to the personal mythology or story held in the molding of his or her face. Yet when
the energy of all these performers fighting for their lives, fighting to
exorcise a virus, or evil spirits, or other dark destructive forces, comes
together, it adds up to a singular mass of explosive, even terrifying, force.
It is for this reason that the witnesses are instructed before this score begins to put on the white masks they found on their seats at the beginning

Warriors in Monster
Dance. Photo © Paul
Fusco/Magnum
Photos.

End of
Monster Dance.
Photographer
unknown.

Witnesses wearing masks for Monster Dance. Photo © Paul Fusco/Magnum Photos.

of the performance, to protect them from the negative force of the Monsters driving directly toward them.

"Witnesses, put on your masks," the narrator instructs. "We need to be protected when the Warrior lines come forward, pushing the danger out. Witnesses, put on your masks. We need to be protected when the carriers break through, carrying the poison out. Witnesses, put on your masks. We need to be protected." The witnesses then form a menacing wall of white impersonal masks that the Monsters must face as they come forward. I chose to use these masks to protect the witnesses as well as to inspire the Monsters. When the performers see the wall of witness masks in performance, it is a surprise, something they have not seen before, and it heightens the intensity of the moment.

"It was a white bank with all these eyes and no real faces," one of the Monster dancers recalls. "I could just give the Monster to them, and they could take it. I didn't know who I was giving it to. It wasn't personal, but we were all there with one another, together." The power of the witnesses is revealed to the performers when the witnesses don their masks. They become another entity involved in the life-and-death struggle enacted by the dance. They become part of the *Circle the Earth* community, dancing with life on the line.

As the three scores merge and come to a close, the Warriors, Monsters, and witnesses converge to create a single confrontation in the space. The Warriors stand next to the Monsters, who have collapsed at the feet of the witnesses. There is often weeping at this time. Everyone is held in an intimate space for that moment, which continues into the next section of the dance.

Involving an audience in our confrontation in such a direct manner invites them into the collective in a visceral way. Not only are they there to witness our actions, but we have chosen to protect them as well, a gesture that reflects their importance to us on both a human *and* a collective level. I cannot say this often enough: the role of the witness is crucial in this dance. It is part of what makes change possible.

For me, the Monster Dance has a special significance. Several months after my cancer operation, I began to work with Dr. Robert Hall to deal with my emotional experiences about the operation. I came to him one day with a dream. I was on the operating table surrounded by six people in long white coats, caps, face masks, and white gloves. They were all white and faceless and inhuman-looking. They were mechanically cutting away at my body bit by bit, piece by piece. I started to scream: STOP! STOP! STOP! but they continued their job as if they did not hear me. I became more and more panicked and desperate, but still there was no response from them. They just kept cutting. When I acted out my dream, the words "STOP IT!" triggered such intense fear that I felt I had gone mad. All the outrage and desperation came surging out of me like an erupting volcano: "Please don't harm my body. Dear God, please don't harm my body. This is my dancer's body and if you harm my dancer's body, what will become of me?" This dream and my cry for help were the beginning of my own Monster Dance.

After the performance, many of the Monster dancers underline the significance of this score. "In all the rehearsals, I would just walk through this part of the dance, and I stayed inside my great fear of being powerless," one man recalls. "Everyone around me was screaming and pushing and fighting, and I just couldn't do it. I wasn't getting out of this bad feeling of mine. And then the night of the performance, I broke through the first two lines, and then when I was behind the last line, I said to myself, 'You're not going through until something happens.' I saw how I had all these people around me, that they were all there for me. I've always felt alone, and I saw then that I am not alone. I have this one chance in my life, and I am going to use it. I don't know what happened, but I pushed through that last line, and when I came through, I felt that I was very powerful. Breaking through that barrier helped me see that life doesn't have to just be about barriers, or struggle. I felt that I left something behind that last line of Monsters, something I had been carrying with me my whole life."

Another reports, "In the Mask Dance I got in touch with my fears. The whole attempt, the mask and the contortions and the expressions and the gestures I conveyed through the Mask Dance, was a way of releasing the evil spirits from my body. And after crossing the gym floor, there was also the whole process of breaking through the Warriors, feeling them, and pushing through them. They gave me support in the sense that I felt their strength, the strength of the Warriors, and I took a lot of that into my body to help me purge the bad feelings and fears and sorrows out of my body."

Yet another says, "My Mask Dance was a Warrior Dance—a dance where I moved from the place of victim to the place of empowerment."

RELEASE AND RESTORATION

The next part of the dance correlates with the stage of release in the Five Stages of Healing. Although there are moments of release throughout the workshop process, the effect of unveiling our fears and our monsters in the performance, to people outside our closed circle, often brings the biggest release. After the expenditure of physical and emotional energy in confronting the dark side during the Monster and Warrior Dances, the performers must have an opportunity to recover. We must take the time and space to solidify the genuine emotions that arise from facing difficult truths. The participants with life-threatening illnesses are given the chance to surrender and yield to the reality of their circumstances. The Monsters allow themselves to be very vulnerable at this time. Many are crying and want to be cared for. They have asked specific people to be their caregivers at this time. Their receptivity to being helped takes a great deal of humility and personal vulnerability. It is also the first time the caregivers in the dance are given the opportunity to demonstrate their compassion for their partners. This is a moment of surrender, both to the desire to nourish and the need to be held. It is about giving and receiving unconditional love. It is, quite literally, a touching moment.

Here is the performance score:

1. Warrior: move to the person who has selected you as the caregiver.
2. Kneel beside your partner, place a hand on your partner's body, and feel her or his breath. Wait until the breathing calms.

Beginning of
Restoration.
Photographer
unknown.

3. When you notice that your partner has recovered from the
   Monster Dance, lift him or her to a seated position. Hold your
   partner so he or she can rest.
4. Begin to sing the Restoration Song with the others.

Restoration Song
Here are the words of the song:

RESTORE ME. RESTORE ME.
In gratitude, the Spirit sings.
The song is a song of thanks.
Restore me. Restore me.
The promise of life is restored.
RESTORE ME. RESTORE ME
Restore my breath. My breath restored.
Restore my blood. My blood restored.
Restore my back. My back restored.
Restore my bones. My bones restored.
Restore my legs. My legs restored.
From head to toe, restore me.
Restore my eyes. My eyes restored.
Restore my heart. My heart restored.

Music for
Restoration Song.
Score © Carol
Swann.

The promise of life is restored.
Restore my seed. My seed restored.
Restore my womb. My womb restored.
RESTORE ME. RESTORE ME.
THE PROMISE OF LIFE IS RESTORED.
Restore my balance. My balance restored.
Restore my trust. My trust restored.
Restore my feelings. My feelings restored.
Restore my faith. My faith restored.
Restore my hope. My hope restored.
Restore my joy. My joy restored.
Restore my relations. My relations restored.
The promise of life is restored.
RESTORE ME. RESTORE ME.
THE PROMISE OF LIFE IS RESTORED.
Restore my sisters. My sisters restored.
Restore my brothers. My brothers restored.
Restore my children. My children restored.
The promise of life. The promise of life.
THE PROMISE OF LIFE IS RESTORED.
Restore my Earth. My Earth restored.
From land to land, restore me.
Restore my Water. My Water restored.
From sea to sea, restore me.
Restore my Sky. My Sky restored.
From Heaven to Earth, restore me.
RESTORE ME. RESTORE ME.
THE PROMISE OF LIFE IS RESTORED.[13]

The Restoration is a key moment in the dance, offering a return to our natural rhythm, to the heartbeat and the breath. After confronting the Monster, everyone needs some time to come back to him- or herself, to arrive at a quieter place, and to balance the confrontation with the dark side with an alliance with the light. This is a time of transformation in *Circle the Earth*, a time to find a balance between intensity and calm. It is a time when the two halves of the equation become whole, when it is clear

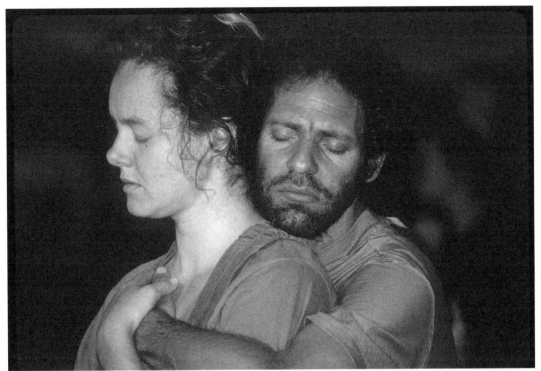

Restoration Dance. Photographer unknown.

that life and death are in a dynamic relationship with each other, and that our experience of one is always affected by the other.

One of the Monster dancers later reflects, "The Restoration was incredibly important at that point because of the sense of alienation and loneliness that I was feeling. I was left feeling in a sense without any direction, without a place to go. And with the first touch of the Restoration came a sense of being able just to be and to receive, to be nurtured, to be touched, to be supported without having to be anything other than what I was in that moment."

A caregiver notes: "This dance made me look at trust, at need, at giving someone what they need while they let go of what they don't. I felt replenished by being able to share that with my partner—he could see something in me that allowed him to go further, and I was able to be there with him in a place that had nothing to do with ego. It had to do with heart, and hope. We can learn to love one another. We can heal some of our pain even if it's just for a moment. The moment is all we have."

The Restoration is also an important moment for the witnesses, who, after watching the unrelenting force of the Warriors and Monsters, are given a chance to catch their breath and be restored with an image of connection. I remember looking at the audience at one point during this section and noticing that many people were holding hands. As the friends

The Bridge.
Photographer
unknown.

and families of people in the dance, the witnesses also need this moment of recovery from the revelation of the dark side. The support of the witnesses is part of what makes it possible for people who are facing a life-threatening illness to continue to live. The collective recognition that *we all need each other to heal and to live* is one of the most powerful parts of this dance.

The importance of community in healing and regeneration comes out in one dancer's remarks: "After the Monster Dance I have exhausted all my feelings. I am then comforted by others and am able to experience a reaffirmation, a kind of rebirth, being led from the period of darkness that the mask represents into an experience of relationship. I am physically tired from expending that energy, and it takes some time for me to be restored after that expression of death and pain and sorrow. Then we are led through a bridge of people who chant, 'Restore me.' All of this makes it possible for me to feel my changes."

The Bridge

As described earlier (see day 7), the next score—the Bridge—provides a transition from release and restoration into a rejoining with the larger group and a movement toward change. From lying down to sitting to standing to moving forward, an energy grows as people form a bridge and move through the shape they have formed. There is an experience of connection among all the dancers who create and walk through the bridge. They are shifting from the private experience of the partners in the Restoration score to a collective experience of community. One dancer speaks eloquently about the function of the Bridge: "This is a place in the dance where we are given a chance to heal our broken relationships with one another and with the earth, and as this begins to shift, we can shift our attention from our own personal pain to the suffering of the earth and begin to dance and sing for her restoration." In performance, participants often begin their walk through the Bridge slowly and with great heaviness, holding one another. Gradually, as they pass one another, they gain more lightness and levity, until their walk becomes jubilant, celebratory, and joyous.

CHANGE

After the peace of the Restoration and the transition of the Bridge, we reach another turning point in the dance, standing at the threshold of a new vision. This is the moment when some completion in our healing journey becomes possible. It is a time when we begin to see new options both in our beliefs and our behaviors. It is not enough to content ourselves with the *possibility* of change; we need to move on to the place where changing will take us, to begin to change with the changing. Questions about integration and the consequences of our dance ritual arise at this point, leading us hopefully to the new world we wish to create through dance and the Life/Art Process. This is a difficult and important part of the cycle, where healing becomes not just another thing to do, but a way of life. Change is the hardest thing to make happen. It is easier for us to identify the conflict than it is for us to actually change it. In the dance, we have recognized our circumstances, named them, and grieved with them. Now we have the opportunity to stand in a new relationship to them. As the leader of the dance, I find this to be a delicate and exciting moment, one that challenges me to use all of my resources in ways that can apply to the situation at hand.

Here is a wonderful story of how change begins to happen, and how the experience of dancing in a group of people facilitates this change. One day toward the beginning of a workshop, when we are doing some vigorous dancing, somebody's head flies off and lands on the floor in front of me. At least, that is how it seems. Actually it is a wig. I stand frozen with surprise and wait to see who will claim it. A heavyset woman walks forward. I can't tell how old she is. She's one of those people who I imagine looks older than they really are, worn down by years of living. I kneel down to hand it to her and our eyes meet. She looks frightened and uneasy. I touch her hand for a moment and say very softly, "It's all right." I notice she has bald spots all over her head and little tufts of hair, and I think she must be having chemotherapy. But I am wrong.

We take the time for J to tell us her story. She says that her father sexually molested her until she was twelve years old, when he stopped. That's when she started pulling out her hair. Her mother would try to stop her by tying her hands behind her back. J is large, wears black baggy clothes, and has a plain face, but when she tells her story, she looks like a tiny child, tormented and helpless. I have an urge to rush to her side and hold her in my arms and comfort her, but I know this will only alleviate my pain, not hers, so I remain still.

The moment of silence following her story seems interminable. Finally, I thank her for letting us in on her secret. The people in the group seem both shocked and deeply moved. I look around at everyone to get a clue of what to do. They all have an expression that cries out: "We want to be your friend. We want to help you." She hasn't put her wig back on yet and she looks strange, but no one pulls away. People are leaning forward to get closer, to catch every word and gesture.

I say, "J, we all want to support you. Tell us what we can do." With hesitation and some quiet thought she says, "If people want, they can stroke my head or rub my belly." From time to time during the week, I watch people with J, stroking her head or rubbing her belly. She never puts her wig back on, not even for the performance, in front of one thousand people. That's a good example of hard-won, embodied change.

Another unforgettable moment that speaks to change occurs in the performance. N, one of the performers with HIV, has not told his parents that he has tested positive. He invites them to fly from Southern California to San Francisco to see him in the performance. He calls them repeatedly to make sure they are taking him seriously and are, in fact, going to be there. They come, bringing his sister as well. What is stunning is the fact that he informs them about his HIV status through the dance. The narration accompanying the "I Want to Live!" score is: "Only those with life-threatening illnesses will come down this path." When N calls out his name and says, "I want to live!" his family knows for the first time that he is infected with the virus.

Later, they tell me how shocked they are. They cry throughout the performance, but by the end, they join the community in the Victory celebration. In a short hour and a half, they go through the same journey N goes through in the dance. They are left, as N tells me later, with a feeling of strength, support, and faith. A month after the performance, the whole family goes on a wonderful vacation trip, something they have never done before. N says, "My relationship with my parents is much more open than it has ever been. We don't spend time on extraneous garbage. When I feel like I need something, I ask for it. For the first time, I feel really connected and very much in the middle of things I think are worthwhile." This speaks to the possibility of change for both witnesses and performers inherent in a ritual like *Circle the Earth*.

The Earth Run

The Bridge takes us into the Earth Run, the pivotal and central score evolving from all the iterations of *Circle the Earth* from the very beginning of its history (see chapter 4 for a detailed description of the score). The Earth Run is an act of commitment. One by one, the participants all stand and dedicate themselves to a specific purpose. Then, they run their intentions in concentric circles within the square of the four directions.

When we do the Earth Run in performance, however, it is somewhat different from the score within the *Planetary Dance*. The context of this score, as part of a larger dance done in front of witnesses, lends a new meaning to the Earth Run relative to the Five Stages of Healing. On the mountain, the Earth Run is a score that connects us to the mountain and to others doing this dance in other parts of the world. As part of the performance of *Circle the Earth*, the Earth Run is a step in the evolutionary process of healing, connecting us to the earlier stages of identification, confrontation, and release, and catapulting us toward new possibilities.

At the beginning of the dance, performers call out "I want to live!" As the dance evolves, they (and their caregivers) are able to say to one another: "And I want you to live." Each person now runs for the life of another. This is an expansion of our personal desires to encompass our hopes for our families and our communities and our world. By running in unity, our purpose is strengthened and our prayers are magnified. We run for those who are in need, for the homeless and the hungry and the abused. We run for those who are no longer with us and for those who struggle with illness. We run for the health of our bodies and the health of the planet herself. One participant says, "I begin the Earth Run by saying, 'I run for my health and the health of all of us.' By that point, my energy has been restored and I circle the gymnasium, running, and in the running process, find a new source of strength and energy."

One HIV-positive participant tells the following story: "I lost my family and what I have been experiencing is grief. My wife was so frightened by AIDS that when I came home from the hospital, she thought I was going to die around her and the children and she left me. I realized I had to begin my life again. My highest moment was the Earth Run, where I ran for my children. I haven't seen them for nine months and I wanted them to know that I love them and care about them and miss them, and that they are a part of my life."

Another dancer reports, "I was very aware that every step of my feet was indeed a prayer. And I felt that through the soles of my feet up through the top of my head." Yet another says, "I was able to let go of the audience and focus on the other participants and on the energy. I was so impressed with people's stamina. I was so moved by what people were running for. I would be running in the circle and as I would be running I would hear somebody standing up and yelling out. I was amazed by the energy level and I was happy for myself that I was able to run so much. I just couldn't get over the strength and stamina coming from a lot of people who were sick."

The Earth Run is unique in the dance. It's the first time that everybody is doing the same thing at the same time in the same place in a very defined pattern. Although we're not all dancing for the same thing, everybody is dancing for something that's so real in his or her life that it matters.

Sound Spiral

In between the Earth Run and the Sound Spiral, everyone stops in one of the four directions for a brief rest. Having reinforced their commitments to change with their feet, the performers now add their voices, humming as they move, spinning and spiraling out, faster and faster, with the sound opening out as well. As we do the Sound Spiral score (see day 7) in the performance, we all move like a whirlwind toward the witnesses, spinning away from the center to take word of our change out into the world. Then we stop, place our fingertips on our hearts, take a deep breath, and release our breath from the heart in a loudly whispered "Pah!" We have circled the earth, we have danced with life on the line. As one participant describes it: "I feel like the 'Pah!' says, 'Here we are. We just gave you a gift. And this gift will keep on giving because it will affect your life. What starts in this dance isn't going to end here.'"

While we do the Sound Spiral, the ceremonial feather is run out of the gym. This is symbolic of taking the word of what has happened in the dance into the wider world.

Victory Dance

The intention of *Circle the Earth: Dancing with Life on the Line* is to break the circle of fear, isolation, and prejudice surrounding the AIDS pandemic, and to create a circle of trust, peace, and compassion. Some of this work takes place through the process of the workshop, as participants gain compassion for each other and learn to love across the borders that separate us. Some of the work happens in the act of performance itself, as those of us who have worked together for nine days share what we have learned with our wider community.

To facilitate the goal of our coming together, at the end of the performance I invite people in the audience who are facing a life-threatening illness, or have a friend or loved one living with AIDS or cancer, to come forward to the floor where we are performing, to form an inner circle and sing the Restoration Song with the participants of the dance. The performers form a bridge, encouraging the witnesses to make the transition to new possibilities, just as they did for themselves earlier in the performance.

The bleachers empty as people come down to join us. As the performers begin singing the Restoration Song and swaying, the witnesses join in, too. The singing, the swaying, the tears, the embracing, the laughter, and the dancing go on for more than an hour. There is great joy as everyone celebrates together; it is like a victory party. This joining of witness to dancer is part of the healing power of any ritual, which is done in service to the larger community.

The facilitators initiate the "Snake" Dance (see day 1), with performers joining hands in a number of lines. Designated leaders lead them in swirling patterns across the floor, taking care to avoid collisions. After some time, as the music slows down and grows quieter, the leaders bring the dance to a closure in a series of circles.

Through this kind of closure, the friends and families of the performers have a chance to make connections nonverbally and on a deeper emotional level than if the dance were to end after the applause, with everyone leaving on their own. Several witnesses tell me later that they were shaken up by the raw emotions of the performance, and they needed the Restoration Song and the Victory celebration with everyone to reorient themselves. One of the participants says, "It was wonderful when the witnesses left the bleachers and came to be with us. It was overwhelming, like having my day-to-day life coming down on the gym floor. I had to integrate all of that, right there on the spot, after being in this closed community of the workshop and performance. I noticed how many boundaries were broken and I felt the boundaries between my intimate life and my public life shifting. It was affirming to have people who know and love me come down and be with me and to have friends who said, 'This was so important for all of us.'"

Another dancer exclaims, "Love just filled that room. It was a wonderful moment. It was a time when I could look to the witnesses and see my family, my grandson and my daughter and my friends. To have something I could share with the people I love was enough." Yet another participant says, "The end when the audience came to join us was the high point of the performance for me. I felt that they had understood our message and that our community had grown bigger. I had such a sense of completion and exhilaration. In a sense, I was fully present and visible for the first time in my life. I said what I needed to say with a group of people. We said something together. I felt exhilarated and deeply peaceful because now my life is really fulfilled. Anything else is a bonus."

CLOSURE OF THE PERFORMANCE

After the Victory Dance, we begin to dismantle the set in a way that shows our appreciation for the witnesses' contributions. Several people from each support group gather the food and flowers from the altars and give them to the witnesses, socializing and thanking them for their support. This closing score allows everyone who participated in the dance—performers and witnesses alike—to share a final moment together. The gift-giving formalizes the reciprocity of the relationship between the witnesses and the performers. The witnesses give the gift of their attention; the performers give the gift of their truth; the flowers and food on our altars are symbols of this shared expression of love.

PROVIDING A ROUTE BACK TO DAILY LIFE

The first time we do *Circle the Earth: Dancing with Life on the Line*, in 1989, the workshop ends with the performance. But when we do it again, in 1991, we add another day, as many of the original participants express a need for more closure. As one dancer tells me: "I didn't have any idea when I agreed to participate what was going to be happening to me emotionally. When I went back to work on Monday, I was a basket case. I shouldn't have been there. I was so raw. Someone would look at me cross-eyed and I would start to cry. I'd be walking down the street and I'd burst into tears because I'd remember something from the week. And that really took me probably a couple of weeks to try to get some kind of emotional footing back and stop being so raw. But now every time I think of that week what keeps coming back to me is the T-shirt that a friend of mine had made for me that says: 'I dance to be alive.' Because that's truly what it feels came out of the week for me. Now I know what my dance is about. My dance is to be alive. And I'm going to continue dancing in all the ways in my life."

Ritual creates an opening, a door through which we can experience a kind of communication different from and deeper than our ordinary day-to-day consciousness. Just as we need time to prepare ourselves to enter ritual time and space, so we must take equal care in leaving it, making ourselves ready to return to our everyday lives. Creating both personal and collective closure to a dance like *Circle the Earth* is especially crucial because we live in a culture that offers little social support for community ritual. The community we create in *Circle the Earth* is a temporary one, and while we are changed by it, the day-to-day world to which we return often is not. We must find ways to mark this reality and live with it, and then we must find ways to integrate our experience of community and support, and apply it to our daily lives.

When we add a closing day, we meet on the morning following the performance to dismantle the rocks and to do our second self-portraits. We find that taking time to meet together as a group once the performance is over helps us integrate this experience with the rest of our lives. This day of closure facilitates the crossing we now have to make: from the ritual world to the secular world. One participant says, "The day after the performance was a time for me to discover what I had learned and to take it home with me instead of leaving it in the gym." As we have clearly learned from our first workshop, when people do not have the chance to incorporate their experience of such a powerful movement ritual into daily life, the effects can be disorienting and the impact of the dance can be dissipated. Since we are really trying to create an efficacious ritual and not just a "good performance," taking time for this incorporation is very important.

As the participants enter the space, they go to their rocks and we do a guided meditation focusing on whatever it is the rocks have to say to us. Now that we have gone through the performance, has the symbolism of the rocks changed? We question what we have learned and gained by doing the dance and we return to some of our initial questions: Who am I? Who are we? What are our values as a community? What is the mystery of life and death? To find those answers, I ask the participants to recall how they performed the dance and how they felt in their lives. I focus their attention with questions like: What did you do in the dance? How were you in relationship to others? Did you lead in the Vortex? Make contact? Follow? Withdraw? How did you perform this dance and how does that match how you are in your life? How is it different? What did you like? What had meaning? I encourage a metaphoric understanding of their dance experiences as a way to apply this dance to their daily lives.

We do this for about forty-five minutes and something amazing happens. Several people are sitting directly behind the rocks that hang suspended from the ceiling by a rope. The rocks are resting at the same level as their hearts. As they sit and reflect on their experience, the rocks start rotating in a small circle in front of their hearts, around and around and around. In some mystical traditions, this ability to make a hanging object move in this way is called dowsing and is often used as a method of divining answers to important questions.

After we finish this silent time, each person selects a piece of paper for a closing self-portrait drawing. Almost everyone chooses paper large enough to do a life-size portrait. They have grown bigger through the process of the dance. After they do these drawings, people share them with their support groups. A highlight of the workshop is comparing the first and last self-portraits and becoming aware of the journey each individual has made. We are able to see the uniqueness of each person's mythology and its connection to the mythology of the collective. One person speaks of his original drawing, which was dark and filled with grief and anger. His final drawing represents the ways he has come to terms with his situation. It is, in his words, "a drawing of a very peaceful place and a very peaceful person."

Noting the differences and commonalities between the beginning and ending self-portraits gives participants an opportunity to talk with each other and to summarize their experiences of *Circle the Earth*. One participant says, "On the first day of *Circle the Earth*, we were asked to draw pictures of ourselves. When I was finished, I was not happy with it. There were parts of it that just weren't what I wanted to see. On the last day, we drew ourselves again, and we were able to discuss the changes in the drawing with the people in our support group. The changes were incredible! In every case, the people in my support group were much stronger. The drawings were happier, more alive. The transformation was phenomenal, and to see how it was embodied, physically, spiritually and emotionally in the drawings was very exciting." Although it isn't possible to make one statement about this closing series of self-portraits, what seems to be true is that after the workshop and performance process, the work of the participants reflects a greater sense of color, integration, and connection to the environment, as well as a sensitivity to their inner worlds.

We end with a prayer written by Allan Stinson: "The spirit of the well is deep. The well of the spirit is deeper still. May the spirit that brought us together keep us together and keep us well along the way." We speak the prayer and we dance it. Then we go to the ocean and feast and celebrate together.

Our time outdoors at the ocean reconnects us to an enduring source of connection and spirituality. As we hike back from the beach, people are

As you bring your community ritual to a close, consider these questions:

What kind of context can you create after the dance is done to help people integrate the experience into their daily lives?

What questions might you discuss with participants to help them reflect on the journey they have taken?

How might you use drawing, writing, or other activities to enhance this reflection?

encouraged to share with each other the changes within themselves they have experienced during this week together and how these changes may affect their lives. We say good-bye to one another at the end of our hike—which ends our time together as this particular group. It is so important for us to mark the experience we have had together, which at times has been difficult and frightening, but which has been ultimately about the creation of human relationships across all the barriers that divide us. Our time at the beach is a pleasurable and memorable way to acknowledge our experiences with one another.

THE IMPACT—ASSIMILATION INTO DAILY LIFE

Once the performance is over, assimilation comes through the ways in which we organize our lives and our art around the changes we have experienced. This is the hardest part of the healing process. This book is, in many ways, a tribute to all the men and women who have taken a healing process into their bodies and their lives and have let themselves be changed. This is a courageous and difficult thing to do. The healing process is circuitous and long. Many of us get stuck identifying the "problem" and never find a solution or take action. What is remarkable about the process and the people who participate in it is the progressive manner in which our discoveries are applied to our lives and facilitate real change. I want to tell you some of the stories of how the people in this dance used what they learned through the process of *Circle the Earth: Dancing with Life on the Line* to come to grips with their living and their dying.

In the workshop, W—who is in the advanced stages of AIDS—is often irritable, cantankerous, and rebellious. During one exercise he stands up and shouts, "You murderers, you murderers," as he waves his arms in the air angrily. I am stunned and confused, but know that, as a workshop leader, I have to find a way to work with him without judgment. His support group stands behind him and I place my hand on his sternum and ask him to fall back into the arms of his group. Without hesitation and to my relief, he does. The group begins to sing the song from the Restoration dance and, as the group gently sways with him in their arms, he looks up at me, winks, and says, "It's working." The exercise allows him to relax and release his hostility, so he can begin to accept the inevitability of his death with something other than rage.

With that change of heart, W devises a way to apply what he has learned from dancing *Circle the Earth*. Here is what he does. One of the women in the group brings her six-month-old baby to the workshop and dances with her child. Many in the group are drawn to the chance to cradle, comfort, and mother this infant. W is one of those who grows to love the child, and often I see him holding her. After the group disbands, he stays in touch with the mother and her daughter. One day he tells me that he is the daughter's godfather and they are going to conduct a ceremony to make it official. He says, "I will be her spirit godfather, her angel, and when I die I will look after her and protect her wherever I am." He has found a way for the dance to continue even after his death.

Circle the Earth gives us not only a common experience, but also common tools and a common vocabulary. As a group, we learn how to use the creative process—the Life/Art Process—to create a context for the events in our lives, to help us find our places in the midst of life's mysteries, and to begin to make sense out of something as senseless as the illness or early death of a good friend. Many participants in the workshop acknowledge afterward that the tools they have gained—access to their bodies, the resource of visual images, and the mental and spiritual associations these realms hold for them—are tools they can integrate into their daily lives and use over and over again. The process of reclaiming the symbols of the body and the mind serves participants long after the dance has ended.

After the performance of *Circle the Earth*, the Positive Motion group of men challenging HIV meets for its own closing event. N arrives and immediately collapses into someone's arms. He is devastated. His best friend has just died and he is preparing to go to the funeral that day. He tells us he almost didn't come to our gathering, but at the last minute decided he wants and needs to be with the group. What can we do to support N? What ritual, ceremony, words, or song can help him? I think of Trails, the score we did on our first day together, and wonder if we could adapt that to N's needs. It is an experiment.

It begins as a visualization: "Imagine you are on a trail on Mount Tamalpais and this trail takes you on a journey. That journey is your life with your friend—all the memories of what you did together, and how you felt when you were together. Imagine as you move along the trail that you are reliving your life with him ..." We form a human trail with our bodies. N closes his eyes and begins his journey. As he goes through the trail he stops at each person as if he is remembering another experience with his friend. When he gets to the end of the trail, he has an expression of great sadness, tears streaming down his face. Then he breaks loose, runs outside, hollers to the sky, and throws up his arms as if to release his friend. When he returns to the studio, he feels very peaceful and strong, and ready to prepare for his friend's funeral. The resource of the group, along with all we have learned about our bodies and our experience through *Circle the Earth*, serves N and the whole Positive Motion group after the performance.

The HIV-positive women who participate in *Circle the Earth* find their own sense of closure, but have to walk through another ring of grief to get there. At Women with Wings' first session after *Circle the Earth*, everyone present has participated in or witnessed the ritual. But C—one of the founding members of the group—is not there. She had become ill during the first days of the workshop and was hospitalized. During the Earth Run, one of the women dedicated her run to C. But it is only when all the women gather together for a regular meeting that the real impact of her absence is felt. All the fears and emotions that have gone unacknowledged during the flurry of the workshop and performance come pouring out.

The issue is raised very simply when one woman acknowledges that it doesn't seem right to begin without speaking of C's absence. And so the women speak of it, and what comes out is an immense feeling of discouragement. It is as if the dance didn't mean anything at all. We all feel depressed and defeated. We created the dance to honor courage and it feels as if there is no courage and no honor. One woman folds her arms and sits in a corner and says, "I'd just as soon die and get it over with now." I am scared and grieved. I think then that I have fooled myself, and that the whole dance is a sham.

And then something shifts. I realize that doing the dance doesn't mean we have to feel good, or be victorious, or conquer our enemy every second of every day. Those feelings are part of the outcome of the dance, but our genuine accomplishment is that we have learned to be true to whatever we feel in the moment. We can be true to ourselves, without judging our experiences, and if that means being discouraged and depressed, that's real. We give ourselves permission to experience fully the whole range of our lives, knowing we have the support and encouragement of loving friends around us. It is as if we say to ourselves: "I can be tired and sad. I can cry. I can ask to be held. I can go and hold you. I can listen to my

---

After your community ritual has ended, consider these questions:

How do you support your group members in the assimilation process?

What is your own personal valuaction of the ritual, the group, and your leadership team?

If you were to do it again, how would the process be different and how would it be the same?

---

friend say, 'I'm going to die and just get it over with,' and I can empathize with her."

This realization helps me during that session, which seems to go on for hours and hours. And through our doubt and our fear, we stay together as a group. It is the one thing we know we can do. It isn't OK to go off on our own and be sad. As a group, we draw a picture and we write poems. We cry and hold each other. It is dark in the room that day. And then we go outside and rest, and suddenly L says, "Come on. Let's get off our asses and dance. We've done enough grieving for now." The next thing I know, we are dancing together and feeling good and laughing and joking. We are doing the only thing we know and, somehow, it's working. We end the session feeling calmer and more peaceful.

When I wonder whether or not a dance like *Circle the Earth* can have any impact on the world, I like to think of this story about Isaac Stern. During the Persian Gulf War, he was playing his violin with the Israeli Symphony in Jerusalem when suddenly the alarm sirens went off. It was well known by the populace that Iraq had missiles pointed directly at Israel, and specifically at Jerusalem. The sirens frightened the audience, who reached under their seats and put on their gas masks. The symphony members quietly and deliberately walked off stage, but Isaac Stern continued to stand, and he continued to play. The audience, with their gas masks on, continued to listen. Afterward, Stern said this was the first time in his life that he felt his music was useful. I see his action as comparable to our dancing through our fear and our grief. Even if the action unfolds in the midst of turmoil of every sort and seems to have no direct impact, our attitude toward it holds the strength and promise of the human heart, of the human longing to be free.

In speaking of the changes he experienced, one participant summarizes what I feel is the powerful potential of this kind of dance ritual: "I began to see myself in a more honest fashion. I began to judge myself a little less and I began to deal with the emotions that come up from having a life-threatening illness. I had to deal with a lot of sadness and a lot of fear and a lot of anger during the process of *Circle the Earth*. This was an opportunity to really have some catharsis around those emotions and begin to see myself not as a victim but as an active participant in my healing process. Whether that leads to curing myself is not the question anymore for me: it's about improving the quality of my life and having control over it for as long as I live. I'm glad that I could be a part of this process, and I am beginning to integrate that into my work with children right now. It's exciting. It gives me hope."

The process of *Circle the Earth*, the tears and joys and victories of the participants, has been a great teacher for me. Being witness to the kind of courage it takes to really change your life and your point of view has been healing for me. I have learned that change is circuitous, elusive, mysterious, and hard to compel. We have only this one choice: to try or not to try to change. The processes I have discovered, while valuable in and of themselves, only work when people are willing.

Circle the Earth *has only been danced in its entirety a handful of times in other parts of the world. Two Tamalpa Institute graduates, Dana Swain and Joy Packard, created one of the most involved and important renditions of this dance.*

INTERLUDE:

DANCING FOR PEACE IN LUANDA, ANGOLA

Dana Swain

I lived in Luanda, Angola, as an American expatriate from 2003 to 2007. That's a simple statement that belies the profound experience of entering another culture, and such a radically different one at that. Initially, I witnessed so much that sent my senses and my emotions reeling. I saw people living in conditions of poverty I could not imagine. I saw people without limbs or paralyzed from polio having to beg for money between cars in heavy traffic. I knew the average life expectancy for an Angolan man was forty-five, and that fifty percent of Angolan children died before the age of five. I also saw an indomitable, creative spirit in the connections between family and friends, through an easy humor, and the creativity of song, drama, and dance.

It was the latter that transported me out of my culture-shocked paralysis and moved me into a place of dedication and inspiration. I knew how movement and dance set my heart free, and I felt that if I could connect on that level with people in Angola, I'd be on my way to finding a healing place for them and for myself. But first I had to find a common ground of expression where two cultures might meet, and where art and healing might serve as the medium. I went on a journey in search of such a medium, and I found the Tamalpa Institute.

After completing the Tamalpa leadership training, I felt I had the tools to bring this work to Angola in a Dance for Peace project. *Circle the Earth* and the *Planetary Dance* offered perfect dance scores with which to begin. My intention was to let Angolan youth use their inherent gifts in dance and performance to address issues of peace in their communities.

At the time Angola had recently emerged from a thirty-year civil war, and issues of war and peace were everywhere. As the youth identified within the dance workshop, peace is not just an issue of "not fighting." Peace is about having clean water to drink, electricity, food, and education. Peace is about a respectful community and a government that allows people to do more than survive—it allows them to thrive.

Joy Packard, my peer in the Tamalpa leadership training, worked with me to create the Dance for Peace in Luanda. We used Tamalpa scores and activities throughout the five-day workshop, culminating in a performance on day 6. It was an amazing experience and wonderful success. Joy reflected in her valuaction about the experience: "Working with the physical, emotional, and imaginative realms of expression in movement and art enables cultural differences to come forward as well as transcending them."

When we started working on the dance, we did not have a specific outcome in mind. We only knew we wanted to support the people in Angola with the skills we had. Perhaps we thought of it as an outlet for deeper exploration of issues surrounding peace and community, but since it wasn't our culture of origin, we couldn't predict the outcome. What felt clear, however, was that it would be a meaningful and creative way to engage—both for the youth to engage as a community and also a way for us to engage with them in a deeper way than perhaps was usual for foreigners.

There are of course many issues in trying to organize a dance in a country and community that is not your own. Eunice Ignacio, an Angolan woman nominated for the Nobel Peace prize for her work with peace and conflict resolution issues in Angola, was the first to hear of and approve the Dance for Peace project. She worked with a group called the Development Workshop, which had a commitment to work with youth. DW had developed an organization called Youth Ambassadors for Peace. These youth—mostly between fourteen and eighteen years of age—were trained to go into communities that had held oppositional political positions in the war and facilitate peaceful discussions around those issues. That was the pool from which we received volunteers. Ms. Ignacio assigned an incredibly dedicated and hardworking project manager, João Gilberto, to our project, to help with outreach to this community. João was also instrumental in soliciting volunteers, finding the venue and a caterer who would feed the youth lunch every day during the workshop, getting money for transportation, and obtaining art supplies.

An incredible amount of organizing went into this project. First was the pitch to the Development Workshop. Once it was accepted, I developed a budget and solicited funds. I wrote a business proposal to several large expat companies working in the area; Chevron provided the total $10,000 I estimated would be needed for the project. With Anna Halprin's permission, I developed the workshop day by day to align with *Circle the Earth*. After making my workshop plan, I met with Anna to discuss it and also consulted with Daria Halprin, the director of the

Tamalpa Institute. Their feedback led me to reconsider my original plan and embrace a simpler, more open score that would really bring out the creativity and spontaneity of the group.

I reached out to the expatriate community for volunteers to help. We created a project timeline and task list with owners assigned tasks and due dates. The volunteers were all women, and they were incredibly helpful and insightful in thinking through details one wouldn't antici-pate in the United States (like bringing toilet paper and bottled water every day). They were my additional eyes during the workshop in case something was happening that Joy or I didn't see or weren't aware of. They handed out nametags and took daily attendance. They came early each day to set up, and donated their own supplies when necessary. They fielded questions from the youth when they were in small groups and fed them back to Joy or me so that we could address them. And they were our moral support and witnesses. They loved watching what was happening in the workshop and they mirrored the sense of power and depth that was emerging from this amazing group of youth.

The venue itself was an unoccupied school. The toilets didn't work—there was a barrel of water and a pitcher to flush the toilets with—and the electrical outlets were unreliable. Even the chairs that were sup-posed to be provided were not there initially. But everyone who partici-pated was dedicated and resourceful, and somehow it all came together.

In the five-day workshop, we combined Anna's *Circle the Earth* scores with the Five Stages of Healing to explore and create a final per-formance dance. Each day had a theme—and we discussed, danced, drew images, and did self-reflective journal writing on that theme. Fol-lowing the Five Stages of Healing, the various creative exercises moved from identification of issues, to engagement with those issues, to release and integration, to change, and (hopefully, at some point) transfor-mation. Throughout the process, the youth developed their own inter-pretations of the dance from Anna's pre-existing scores. For example, on the first day we worked on identifying issues in their community, such as lack of security, education, and pollution and garbage prolifera-tion. Then, through the Vortex Dance, everyone found a way of coming together and creating a symbol of their community. They chose to form a baobab tree with their bodies—honoring the role of this tree in Angolan communities as a gathering place for meetings, prayer circles, and sacred ceremonies. The next day we confronted the identified issues and created a Warrior Dance that could fortify participants while engag-ing with those issues.

There were many profound moments during the workshop and performance. On the fourth day of the workshop we let the kids create their own closing ritual. We broke them into groups of ten to create their own dances and share them with the group. Joy and I facilitated a discussion about which parts of the dances they had witnessed would be used in the closing ritual. With fifty kids participating, there was a lot of intense discussion. At one point talks broke down and an argument between two strong leaders in the group ensued, with the rest of the youth taking sides behind these two. This was so reflective of what happens in many conflict situations. We were down to the last five minutes of the workshop—there was pressure to finish on time. I brought to their awareness how the conflict was manifesting, that it was a perfect example of how people get into conflict. I suggested they "move it" rather than talk about it. Within moments, through movement, the conflict was resolved in a dance that blended the ideas of the conflicted parties together. We ended with not one minute to spare, but exactly on time. It was a moment of true triumph and reflected the whole purpose of this work. The youth used the principles they believed in along with creative movement and expressive practices to come to a resolution of their conflict.

All along the way there were unexpected challenges. For example, we had hired musicians to be a part of the workshop and performance, but they never showed up. One youth, Manuel, volunteered to play the African drum throughout the workshop and performance. That single drum turned out to be enough. We didn't have money for props or costumes, so the performers all wore their "Youth Ambassadors for Peace" T-shirts. And, while all the participants could dance naturally, they were not trained in following dance directions, nor were Joy and I experienced choreographers! So we kept it simple, which was no less powerful.

The performance on day 6 was electric. Everything came together. The Earth Run section was particularly amazing. When we practiced it during the workshop, the youth kept running into each other, crowding each other, not moving to the rhythm of the drum—I was at a loss. But, during the performance, they just did it. It was tremendously powerful and the most moving part of the performance. To this day, I don't know what happened, but I suspect they appreciated the importance of the ritual, and they held their prayers and wishes for the actual day, and then the power of their commitment to the dance run was palpable to every witness and to themselves.

One by one the kids went up to the microphone and dedicated their run to the women of Angola, to the children who couldn't afford going to school that year, to adequate health care, and to many other deeply relevant issues. Then, spontaneously, some kids left the run and gathered members of the audience to run with them. At another spontaneous moment the kids ushered their witnesses back to their seats and continued their run. At the end of the run, the kids sat back to back, and two kids who'd had a bit of a rivalry going during the workshop spontaneously spoke out a prayer, one asking for forgiveness, and the other granting his forgiveness. Forgiveness is a powerful, necessary part of peace that naturally manifested for these youth as part of their healing process. In order to heal, first we must forgive and be forgiven.

For the last section of the performance, the transformation, the youth had created their own song. They sang this song with heart and soul. Then, at the end, the young people picked the drummer, Manuel, up off the floor and raised him over their heads in praise and thanks for sacrificing his part in the dance to be the drummer. That was a joyous moment of gratitude and appreciation within their community.

Eunice Ignacio was in attendance on the first day and gave a speech during the Earth Run on the performance day. She brought the directors and creators of Development Workshop to attend the dance, and she was honored by the youth for her support of their work.

My hope had been to give youth in Luanda, Angola, an experience of bonding and of exploring issues of peace in their country. I believe we accomplished that goal, but in addition the youth gave me a gift— one of hope. I was overwhelmed with their dedication, their creativity, openness, vitality, and community. I was really struck by how the youth interpreted the meaning of the dance for themselves. On one level, they began to recognize that true peace was not just about the cessation of war, but also about what resources were available, including clean water and garbage service. One young man even recognized that saying something derogatory to a woman on the street was an act of violence. As another participant, Jindanji, eloquently stated: "Peace is an aspect of living, not just shutting down guns." Everyone thought deeply about what the word "peace" really means, and how that relates to the larger community.

The participants also felt that this dance was full of meaning. They told me they had learned dances as part of their cultural heritage, but because of the war they had lost the connection between the movement of the dance and the meaning of the dance, and that the Dance for Peace brought that connection together again. Some youth wanted to take the dance—particularly the Earth Run—to their communities in the country villages. For a generation, the land mines from the war had separated those in the city from those in the country. They felt the meaning of the dance would help them connect on a visceral level to those who perhaps still retained the memory of the meaning of their cultural dances of origin. Perhaps they felt like the Dance for Peace was a kind of new creation story after a long-lived narrative of destruction.

I had felt compelled to facilitate this project, but at the time I did not question my own drive to do the dance with these youth. Sometimes I wondered what in the world I thought I was doing to take on such a big project, and yet I was totally immersed in the process. The day after the dance I had the insight that my drive to do the dance was my own unconscious need for healing. I was heartbroken to see the devastation in Angola when I arrived there. You can see images of war and its aftermath on the news, but nothing prepares you for the in-your-face reality of it. The dance was the outcome of my own need for healing, and it was transformative for me because I did feel healed in participating and witnessing the beauty, openness, and engagement of these youth. They were a profound inspiration for me. I hope some of them felt even a bit of the transformation and healing that I experienced. And I hope that the project helped the participants find creative tools to manage their differences, new ways to tell their stories, the capacity to engage in a deeper sense of respectful community, and the ability to reclaim pieces of their heritage through dance.

As Joy described the final performance in her journal: "Full of hope, presence, spirited youthfulness, dreams, fun and souls shining ever so brightly.... It was a homecoming. It was a performance. It was a ritual. It was theirs."

Planetary Dance

4

Beyond our immediate community, we are all connected, from country to country. The whole earth is one. In this time of global conflict, economic hardship, and ecological crisis, I believe people need to embrace their connections to each other and the planet and to take a stand for their lives and all they hold dear. The *Planetary Dance* offers people of all ages and abilities a way to come together and take this stand. The *Planetary Dance* is not a pretend experience; it's not make-believe. It's not done for art's sake. It's done to create change. The dance encourages us to find ways that express our inherent connections to each other and to the planet rather than our independence. We need each other, now, in these trying times, more than ever. The *Planetary Dance* provides an experience that reminds us of our oneness, our connection with the earth, and gives us hope that we can learn to live in harmony even when we feel threatened on all sides. It offers us an opportunity to voice our concerns and embody them in a way that impels us to take action. The *Planetary Dance* is both a community ritual and a global dance—it is for all people, everywhere.

At the core of the *Planetary Dance* is the Earth Run—the central score for change in *Circle the Earth*. From the beginning, its power surprised me. In the winter of 1980, while teaching a class in scoring, I wanted to demonstrate the difference between an open and a closed score (see "The RSVP Cycles" in chapter 1). As I walked down the outdoor steps to my studio, I heard the cry of a large black bird and observed its beautiful, effortless movements as it circled overhead. "That's it," I thought. "I'll use circles." For the open score I let the performers choose freely how to move, as long as they used the motif of a circle. The circle served as a way to contain and support their movement. In contrast, for the more closed score, I asked my students to run or walk within a particular pattern of circles, in unison, moving to a steady drumbeat.

When we did the closed running/walking score, I had no expectations about the outcome. I had allotted only fifteen minutes but was startled when the twenty-four students performed the score for close to an hour with intensity and commitment. How was it that running or walking in a circle was so compelling? I was curious about this unexpected outcome. Was the circle pattern an archetypal form tapping into a deeper unconscious place? Did running in unison establish a community bond? Was the run an energizer? Did the power of the collective body enable each person to stretch beyond their personal limits of endurance? I didn't have the answers to these questions, but my curiosity was aroused.

I began experimenting with this score with other large groups. I have learned that each time we do a particular score, it deepens in meaning. The experience of performing it yields more information. Over time this simple running score evolved, expanding and changing with information gathered from each group's performance of it. It was a great example of the recycling process from the RSVP Cycles. The basic, unifying movement of running to the same beat remained the same, but the score expanded to include three circles at different speeds as well as a space in the center to "rest" in one of the four directions. I tried it out in a community dance class for over sixty people after teaching the participants the skills of cooperation required to run in unison. I also offered this score at several conferences with large groups of participants. As the score evolved, I found deeper content, naming it the "Earth Run" and clarifying its intention with a phrase—"each step upon the earth is a prayer for peace and healing."

To reinforce a sense of commitment to the dance, I now asked each person to declare out loud his or her own intention in running for peace and healing. This addition combines an open aspect with the closed score of defined circles and unison running. A participant might, for example, choose to run for her friend Ellen and all others who have been attacked by bullies. In this way each individual connects on a personal level to the larger, collective purpose of peace and healing, both verbally and through action. It allows participants to tap into their deep human longing to be joined with others in unifying movement and intent.

In evolving this score, I was strongly influenced by all that I have learned from Native American dances. In particular, I have always been struck by the power of repetition in native dances. When everybody does the same step at the same time, it creates an energetic force that shifts our awareness. It takes us out of our egos and puts us into a different state of consciousness. Dancing together like this over time taps into the ancient spirit of dance, so we begin to dance for all people everywhere.

As I taught the Earth Run score to new groups in different places, I noticed how moved people were by their dance. In 1987, as described in chapter 2, we expanded the reach of the Earth Run, excerpting it from the longer *Circle the Earth* ritual and inviting people all over the world to lead their communities in a *Planetary Dance* for peace. During the height of the Cold War, Americans and Russians joined together in an Earth Run at an international peace event. For a day of celebration with Native Americans, we framed the dance with Chief Seattle's speech, as a way to honor our country's native ancestors and their relationship to the earth.[14] At the United Nations Plaza in New York, we danced with representatives from four continents and saw the potential global connections implicit in the dance. In 1995, for the fiftieth anniversary of the Potsdam Treaty ending World War II, four hundred people participated in *Planetary Dance: A Prayer for Peace* in the square adjacent to Hitler's bunker in Berlin. Everywhere we offered the dance, I saw new ways that it could serve different groups of people. In Germany and Japan, for example, I learned how issues concerning the local natural environment could guide participants. When one Japanese father was unable to attend our event, he wrote to me describing how he and his son had created their own Earth Run in his backyard. In Australia, the Aborigines incorporated the evocative music of the didgeridoo into a *Planetary Dance* in front of the national government offices. In all these places, I was struck by how the *Planetary Dance* spoke to a central human need—to our need to connect with others and to take meaningful action. This simple dance, which anyone can do, taps into an archetypal form that catalyzes a sense of bonding and commitment.

In sending the Earth Run on its journey around the globe, we do not ask people to imitate what we do on our mountain in Marin County. Instead, we hope that each community will personalize the dance to suit their own needs. Although the Earth Run score is the core of every *Planetary Dance*, each community can choose how the ritual begins, how the participants are prepared, how the group enters the space where the dance is performed, what kinds of instruments or vocals are used to reinforce the steady beat, and how the event ends—all these elements and more are open to adaptation to a particular community's needs and traditions.

What are the key aspects of every *Planetary Dance*? The overall intention is always "peace among peoples and peace with the earth," but each community may choose to focus on a specific issue that is important to them. One year, for our dance on Mount Tamalpais, we named healing from breast cancer as our community intention, as so many women in

Americans and
Russians meet at
Planetary Dance
during Cold War.
Photographer
unknown.

Publicity image for
Planetary Dance.
Photo © John Veltri–
Marguerite Lorimer,
www.earthalive
.com.

our county were struggling with the disease; another year we highlighted
the difficulties our children face. In relation to both the community and
global intentions, each participant also voices a personal intention—what
she or he is dancing for—which really gives this ritual its meaning.

The dance itself calls for simple, everyday movements—running, walking, standing in place, and pulsing to a steady beat. The very simplicity
of these movements makes it possible for any*body* to join this dance.
These movements are contained within a particular spatial architecture.
The outer borders are usually defined by the marking of the four directions—north, east, south, and west. Inside, three concentric circles of
dancers walk or run at different speeds, creating a moving mandala. The
musicians normally stand in the center, so the beat radiates out, toward

the dancers. The clarity of this architectural structure helps to hold the energy of the dance.

Most important, the *Planetary Dance* invites us to align our energies with one another. If we are going to be part of a powerful circle of people running for something we each care deeply about, we need to move our egos out of the way, to give them over to the larger body. What matters is your willingness to commit yourself to your intention and to the larger circle of humanity. There is a Zuni saying: "We do not dance for ourselves, we dance for the life of the community." The *Planetary Dance* takes dance away from its emphasis on individual creativity into a collective form that allows for a creative participation with the energy of all life.

The essential metaphor of the *Planetary Dance* is from the one to the many, which transports us from our individualism to an experience of collective oneness. The constant repetition of the drumbeat and the formation of one circle after another help us see and feel our separate lives in a larger context. By running and walking in unison, and standing for the struggle of others, people are able to experience the possibility of their individual actions influencing the larger whole. As a social species, we need these ceremonies to come together, celebrate our unity, and connect with the larger body of our planet. I believe in dance with purpose, movement with meaning, and a creative method that extends art into everyday life. I hope that the legacy of the *Planetary Dance*, as it continues to evolve, may show us how we can all, as a global community, dance with purpose upon the earth.

AN OPENING CEREMONY

To give a better sense of what a *Planetary Dance* entails, let me describe the one we do on Mount Tamalpais and then mention a few of the hundreds of *Planetary Dances* that have been done around the world. For our dances on Mount Tamalpais, we always start with a sunrise ceremony, arriving at the peak of the mountain just before dawn and watching the day break over a vast landscape below. At the first appearance of the sun, seven Peruvian whistles are blown. These whistles are special reproductions of vessels that people in the Andes made 2,500 years before the Conquistadors arrived. Fabricated from red clay, each vessel is like a sculpture, with a differently shaped body and animal-like face. In the 1970s, after purchasing one of these vessels at a local auction, Daniel K. Stat discovered that the sound he heard from the whistles "forced a sacred connotation which had neither been anticipated nor solicited. It was akin to the mantra—invoking a spiritual, emotional and philosophical harmony

Anna blowing
Peruvian whistle at
sunrise ceremony.
© Jay Graham
Photographer. Anna
Halprin Papers;
courtesy of Museum
of Performance
and Design,
San Francisco.

"Sunrise is for me a very important part of *Planetary Dance*," says
Marguerite Etemad. "For me it is when I prepare myself personally. It is
when I make prayers for myself and connect with nature, grounding myself.
I have witnessed sunrise on Mount Tamalpais about twenty-two times now.
Each sunrise has been unique and there are always special moments—
moments when the hummingbirds swoop and dive around us and
moments of sharing where the resonance is deep and profound."

with the universe."[15] He then painstakingly created his own replicas of
these vessels from clay he collected from different places and distributed
them to certain individuals and communities. One day, I was delighted to
find a set of seven at my front door, and they seemed the perfect vessels
for inaugurating our day of dancing for peace.

After the blowing of the whistles, participants are invited to offer
music, dance, poems, stories, and blessings. We then descend to a trail
just below the peak that loops around the mountain. We take this easy
trail around the peak, stopping for a standing meditation in each of the
four directions.

PREPARING THE PARTICIPANTS

After the sunrise ceremony on Mount Tamalpais, people gather in a
meadow at the foot of the mountain. Before beginning the Earth Run,
people need to be prepared in body and mind to enter ritual space. We tell

Anna explaining
the Earth Run,
2005. Photo
© John Kokoska.

Offering by Justice
Arts Collective,
2016. Photo
© Sue Heinemann.

Writing intentions
on chalkboard,
2015. Photo
© Sue Heinemann.

the story of the dance, and we explain the whole score, using the graphic images that appear in this chapter. Often we invite artists to contribute an offering, such as this spoken-word piece by my grandson Jahan Khalighi:

WE SHOULD DANCE
We should dance

as if dancing were a symbol of peace
as if gyrating arms and fluctuating feet
were the true signs
of an anti-war
movement

We should dance

as if we were standing in a circle of capoeiristas
as if the women of the Zapatista
bandana-covered faces, fists unraveled
just overthrew the United States government
and decided to plant the seeds

of medicinal trees
in the soil
of all our
dislocated
biospheric dreams

We should dance

for the safety of black lives
in these tumultuous times
of stolen sons
and murdered moons
children
taken too soon
targeted
by the color of their skin

We should dance

as if we were kids again
a persistent primordial pulse
pumping within our chest
as if inscribed inside the folds of our flesh
were scriptures of ancient text
and it was only
through dancing
that this hidden
wisdom
could be expressed

We should dance

to shake and wake ourselves
from complacent stupor
for indigenous water protectors
praying on the front lines of our future
singing ancestral songs
into ceremonies of survival

We should dance

as if to make sanctuaries of our bodies
to welcome in the stranger when they have had to flee
people now scuttled like sacred seeds across the sea
for any day you or I could be a refugee

We should dance
like a thousand bursting roses
rising from an Arab Spring

as if the answers were less important
than the burning songs we sing

We should dance

as if it were apartheid South Africa
and Mandela just got released from behind metal bars
as if the earth below
were actually the night sky of another world
and our scurrying feet
were their shining stars

We should dance

to celebrate the sun
as if the earth were alive
and pulsing like a drum
as if the ground were a dream
and movement made it lucid
as if our bodies were shaped
and made for making music

We should dance

as if no one were looking
as if grandma was cooking
as if shedding our skin

We should dance
We should dance
We should dance

More often.[16]

Just as we did each day in the workshops for *Circle the Earth*, we tune
up our bodies for the Earth Run. Often I'll begin by asking the drummer
to give us a beat and then have everyone shake out their bodies to the
beat, getting rid of tension, warming up their muscles, and just having
some fun moving. Then I focus on movement that is central to the dance.
Although the Earth Run uses ordinary movement that almost anyone
can do—running, walking, pulsing—it's important to fully embody our
movements, connecting with the earth and the sky, and feeling this con-

nection through our heartbeat and our breath. Whenever we step down, we need to feel grounded, sensing the earth beneath our feet. As we rise up, we need to feel the opposite, extending toward the sky. The repetition of this down/up movement reinforces our relationship to nature, to the earth and sky around us. We are part of something larger than ourselves.

Tuning Up for the Earth Run

Intention: Get in touch with breath and heartbeat.
                 Feel grounded and uplifted.
                 Move together to a common pulse.

SCORE

Time: 30 minutes or more (depending on group size).
Space: Variable, gathered around leader and drummer(s).
People: All participants.
Activities:

1. Stand with your legs shoulder-width apart. Focus on your breathing. Start by putting your hands on your rib cage and taking a deep breath, feeling the movement there. Then, as you let the breath out, feel the release go into your knees, and allow yourself to drop. Can you feel this in your feet? Listen to what's happening inside your body.

2. Take a partner. First person: stand with legs at shoulder-width and imagine that you are rooted to the earth, visualizing this in your mind. Can you feel the strength of this position? Second person: move behind the first, place your elbows under your partner's armpits, and try to lift your partner straight up. Take care not to pull backward, as that will throw your partner off-balance. If your partner is grounded, you won't be able to lift him or her. Try this again, but this time the person being lifted should think about what you had for breakfast or something equally mundane. Is the person easier to lift now? Switch roles and repeat. Notice the importance of connecting your mind to your intention.

3. Now feel for the sky. Lift up from the sternum and raise your arms out and up, lifting up from the elbows and the scapula. Imagine the movement traveling through the tips of your fingers up toward the sky.

4. From this uplifted position, let out a sound from your belly. This is the embodied sound you want to use when calling out your intention. (See the discussion of Intention below.)

5. Explore the effects of gravity and momentum. Standing with your arms raised up, as in step 3, see what happens if you just let go,

As she drums the pulse for the *Planetary Dance*, Barbara Borden says, "My whole being opens to the connection with everything in the universe that pulsates—which is everything. I realize that I am pulsing as part of the one great heartbeat of life."

into gravity, letting the weight of your head drop you down. Be sure to keep your knees soft, not locked. Come back up and now add your arms as you drop, letting them swing. With momentum, they will take you up again. Experiment with swinging in your own way. This movement will activate the spine and connect the running and walking movements in a natural, relaxed way.

6. Now begin to explore the beat. As the drummer establishes a beat, pulse up and down in place to it, making sure you feel grounded. Have fun with this movement—enjoy it.

7. Hold hands with a partner and turn in a circle as you step together to the drumbeat. Join hands with another couple, continuing to circle to the drumbeat. Keep adding new groups, making the circle bigger and bigger, as you prepare for the circles of the Earth Run.

Training participants to run or walk collectively to the drumbeat is one key to a successful *Planetary Dance*. It is the beat danced together that creates the power in the circle to send our intentions, our calls for action, out into the world.

Additional Preparatory Scores

When I do a preparatory workshop the day before the *Planetary Dance*, I introduce additional scores to support people in fully committing to the run. Here are some useful scores drawn from those preparatory workshops.

KEEPING TIME SCORE

Intention: Cultivate awareness of the pulse.

SCORE

Time: 10–15 minutes.

Space: Large circle.

People: All participants.

Activities:

1. Sit in a circle facing each other.

2. First person: start the beat with a single clap. Next person:

establish the rhythm by clapping another beat. "Pass" the responsibility to clap from person to person around the circle so that each clap is in time with the one preceding it. If someone goes off-beat, laugh and just start again from there. The idea is to have fun, as if playing a game. No one should feel embarrassed at missing a beat (which often happens).

3. Repeat step 2 with a faster or slower pace.

This exercise requires that everyone listen and remain alert to what is going on. The playful aspect of this score delights participants, and although the instructions are easy, the activity requires full attention.

GROUP AWARENESS SCORE

Intention: Move as a group with awareness of those in front of you and behind you.

SCORE
Time: 30 minutes.
Space: Center of space.
People: All participants, divided into two groups: one performing, the other witnessing.

Activities:
1. Performing group: stand close together with left shoulders facing into the center of a circle.
2. Allow a movement to gradually arise, with the group following as one body.
3. Remain focused on each other and slowly expand the circle.
4. Without losing consciousness of each other, let the circle grow to the periphery of the room, then bring it in and close it again.
5. Valuact, with witnesses describing what they saw.
6. Switch roles and repeat.

WAKING UP THE FEET SCORE

Intention: Sensitize feet for walking and running.
SCORE
Time: 30 minutes.
Space: Entire space.
People: All participants (preferably barefoot).
Activities:
1. Sit down and cross one leg, bent at the knee, over the other.
2. Rotate the foot on top at the ankle, in and out, then flex and extend.

3. Shake your foot, switch your leg positions, and repeat with other foot.
4. Place both feet on the ground and claw the ground with your toes.
5. Fan your toes sequentially, starting with your little toe.
6. Standing up, explore shifting weight from the front of the foot, to the back, and from side to side. Find the center of your foot.
7. Lift heel, ball, and toe off the ground in sequence. Rock back and forth, heel, ball, and toe.
8. Bounce in place, using the full range of your feet.
9. Accent the downbeat, then accent the upbeat.
10. Take your explorations into space, feeling heel, ball, and toe touch the ground and experimenting with accenting upbeat and downbeat.

Whenever you dance, you need to be aware not only of your breath, but also of your pulse. In the Earth Run, it is especially important to take your pulse into your feet. You will be pulsing to the beat of the drum with your feet, using every step as a call for peace.

RUNNING SCORE

Intention: Practice running skills.
SCORE
Time: 1 hour.
Space: Circle in center of space.
People: All participants divided into two groups, with one group resting as the other performs.
Activities:
1. First group: stand in a circle, balanced over the center of your feet.
2. Slowly begin to lean forward into a run.
3. Notice the flexibility and bounce in your feet, ankles, and knees.
4. Move your arms and legs in opposition to each other at the same range. When you take big steps, let your arms swing in a larger arc. When you take small steps, bend your arms at the elbows and move them in a smaller arc.
5. Stay in time with the beat, regardless of whether you run with small or large strides.
6. Rest while score is repeated with second group.

This exercise combines physical skills with group awareness and rhythmic sensitivity. Once everyone is running together in unison in a circle, the results are self-generating. The force of this "one body" running inspires the participants, often promoting much greater endurance than any individual run. In directing this score, the leader might offer new resources to the runners. For example, older people or those with physical challenges might start an inner circle of dancers walking to the beat. Fast and energetic runners might start another, bigger outer circle if space allows. Each person is moving at his or her own pace, but adhering to the common beat—an essential skill for the Earth Run.

In both this exercise and the actual Earth Run, when the running or walking begins to build, new patterns can take over. People often begin to improvise—forming new rhythmic relationships based on the common beat and different group formations. This phenomenon is always delightful to witness. It is not breaking the score. Rather, the score establishes a strong commonality, which leads the group into its own signature piece. A new freedom arises, enabling the participants to create their own collective dance and generating a renewed wave of energy that keeps the dance going until it comes to a close of its own accord. I have never witnessed any two Earth Runs done the same way. Each time, each group finds their own signature run.

SETTING AN INTENTION

In addition to warming up our bodies, it's critical to clarify our intentions for the Earth Run. The *Planetary Dance* is always danced for a purpose, an intention connected to the lives of the dancers. All *Planetary Dances* have the broad theme of dancing "for peace among people and peace with the earth," but each *Planetary Dance* also focuses on a particular theme with relevance to the community that dances it. Over the years on Mount Tamalpais we have danced for healing from AIDS and other life-threatening diseases, for an end to gun violence, for restoring our environment, and for protecting our children's future—to name a few themes. Other communities have danced to heal from natural disasters, to bring hope to inner-city communities, or to promote peace between nations.

Beyond the community intention, we each individually commit ourselves to an intention that has personal meaning, to something that we care enough about to run for with all our might. Before joining the run, we each stand and call out who or what we're running for. The act of naming your run in this way is very potent. In certain traditions, naming is a power—naming something creates a forceful energy and signals our determination. Some people know long before the day of the dance what they want to run for; others need time before we begin the run to discover what feels important enough to declare.

Your personal intention is what makes the dance work. It is what will

For a variety of reasons, sometimes people resist trying to find an intention, someone or something to dedicate their run to. Jamie McHugh recalls the resistance he encountered from a choreographer during a *Planetary Dance* facilitators' training he conducted for professional dancers in France in 2012: "When we talked about what was going on, what emerged was that his brother was in the hospital and had said, 'I've always wanted you to dance for me.' I said, 'Sounds like you've got your dedication for the *Planetary Dance*.' 'But,' he said, 'it would make me really emotional to say that, it would throw off my performance.' It was too personal for him to know how to work with.

"I told him it was really up to him what to say in his dedication. We can be as revealing as we want, or not. I said, 'Your emotions are fuel for your dance. This is what propels you. Don't get obsessed with the movement, be more focused on what's moving you.' After we did the dance, this man said, 'That was so amazing. Everything in me came together. My brother, the movement, the form.' Once he was able to acknowledge his vulnerability and move with that, the experiment of running with his feelings, his truth, came together for him. He was so happy to be able to tell his brother that he had danced for him."

propel you into running as long and as powerfully as you can, because you are running for something you care deeply about. Often we have done three runs to allow for three different kinds of intention. The first run is for someone in your immediate life—like your grandmother who has cancer, or a friend who is trying to overcome drug addiction, or a colleague whose house was just destroyed by fire. The second run is for something in the world that you feel strongly about, such as racial justice, or peace in the Middle East, or preventing climate change. Sometimes we have combined these two runs—so you might declare, "I run for my grandmother and all people fighting cancer." The last run is for our children, who are here to carry us into the future.

There are many ways to help people shape their intentions. In recent years we've set up a chalkboard where participants can write or draw their intentions before the run. During our introduction we try to give examples of possible intentions. The idea is to come up with a short, pithy statement that captures the essence of your intent. You might ask, for example: What aspect of working for peace among people and peace with the earth is most important, most real, most present, most engaging for me right now? Is there an obstacle to peace that I can help overcome? Sometimes we ask people to gather in small groups to share their intentions before the run, or we invite a few people up to the mic to voice their commitments to the group at large. Hearing what other people care about can sharpen your own focus.

Here are some poignant examples combining a personal connection with a global one:

> "I run for my son who is schizophrenic, that he find peace in his life, and for all people with schizophrenia."
>
> "I run for my friend who is being evicted from her apartment, and for all those displaced from their homes, that they find a roof over their heads and warmth."
>
> "I run for my friend in Flint, Michigan, who is afraid to drink tap water, and for clean water for people everywhere."
>
> "I run for the safety of my brother serving in the army in Afghanistan, and for the safety of all people in Afghanistan."

I cannot stress enough how important it is to choose an intention that is meaningful to you. As one participant put it: "The act of yelling something out, calling out what you care enough to run for, was really powerful to me. You had to yell that out and then you ran as long as you could because you cared so much about what you were running for."

PREPARING THE SPACE

When we do the dance at the foot of Mount Tamalpais, the initial gathering place and the performance area are in different spaces, occasioning a processional walk from one to the other. After warming up our bodies and setting our intention, we are ready to move to the space where we will do the Earth Run. In recent years I have been developing this transition from our gathering and orientation place (the secular space), to the ritual space where the Earth Run begins. Walking two by two, the drummers lead the way, followed by four flag bearers, each holding a brightly colored red, green, yellow, or purple flag. Then come the participants in pairs, holding hands, proceeding in silence while absorbing the sights, scents, and sounds of the environment around them. At the entrance to the performance space, the musicians move forward, into the center of the space, while the flag bearers split into twos and turn, taking half the participants to the left and half to the right and going around in a large circle, until the two halves meet. The flag bearers then move until one is standing in each of the four directions. This procession may be unique to the Mount Tamalpais *Planetary Dance*, but some kind of transition from a secular to a ritual space is needed to set the tone for the run. I encourage people not only to walk in silence but also to be aware of their surroundings as the dance begins. The procession is done mindfully so it becomes an opportunity for the participants to begin to step into the special time and space of ritual.

Honoring the four directions lends a symbolic resonance to the dance. Just as your body has four "directions" to orient you in space—a top and a bottom, a front and a back—so too does the larger body of the world. By honoring north, south, east, and west, as well as the sky and the earth, we connect our individual bodies to the greater universal body. We share the earth—even though our specific environments are different, everyone has the sky overhead and the earth underfoot. Everyone breathes the air that circulates around the globe and is nourished by the same sun. Through this common experience we can feel our connection to people around the world.

The four directions serve as meaningful symbols across many cultures. In my own Jewish tradition, for example, the symbolism of the four directions can be found during the Sukkot (Harvest) ritual. In one hand, the rabbi holds a palm branch, willow, and myrtle woven together, while in the other hand, a citrus fruit. Ceremoniously, they are shaken in the four directions as well as up and down, acknowledging that God is everywhere. In the teachings, the palm represents the spine, the willow the eye, the myrtle the mouth, and the citrus the heart. The mouth speaks what the heart feels, the eyes truly see, and the spine holds it all together through the integrity of the person.

In Native American traditions, a four directions dance literally shapes the four directions and in that process remakes the world. When we did *Circle the Earth: Dancing with Life on the Line*, Jasper Redrobe Vassau described the symbolism of each direction based on the traditions of his Cheyenne people (see day 2 in chapter 3).

I do not insist on a particular meaning for the four directions, but I believe that marking them in some way can help anchor the circles in which we run. If the symbology of the four directions is not meaningful to you, I encourage you to find your own way to authenticate the space where you will do the Earth Run. Some people simply mark the circle with flour or cornmeal or some other substance that will stay in place for the duration of the run. Others mark the space with banners or other design elements. On Mount Tamalpais, marking the four directions is a clear way to locate us in time and space. I feel it's important to find some way to "locate" your dance that has meaning and import for your community of dancers.

THE EARTH RUN SCORE

The Earth Run is designed to be accessible to anyone, regardless of age or physical prowess. Running, walking, and pulsing to the beat are simple "steps" that most people can easily do. Those who may have difficulty running or walking can be invited into the center to pulse with the musicians.

After entering the space, all the participants stand, hand in hand, in a huge circle, with the musicians and facilitators in the center. Joining together in this way is a symbol of unity, for a circle has no beginning or end; all the points are equally significant. Before the run starts, a horn or a conch shell is blown in the four directions and there is usually some kind of blessing of the site. At times Native American participants, including my grandchildren LeVanna and Micah Vassau, have done a traditional smudging with sage for the children, making them feel special and giving them the message that something important is going to happen. We now acknowledge elders and those with disabilities, ensuring a safe start for them by inviting anyone uncomfortable with running to enter the central area before the dance begins. Then four pre-chosen participants, each situated in one of the four directions, lead off the run, offering their dedications as well as modeling the run and establishing the pace.

Intention:	Dance with a purpose for others.
	Become one with the earth and each other.
SCORE	
Time:	As long as it takes—until the dancers tire.

Earth Run score.
Graphic design by
Stephen Grossberg.

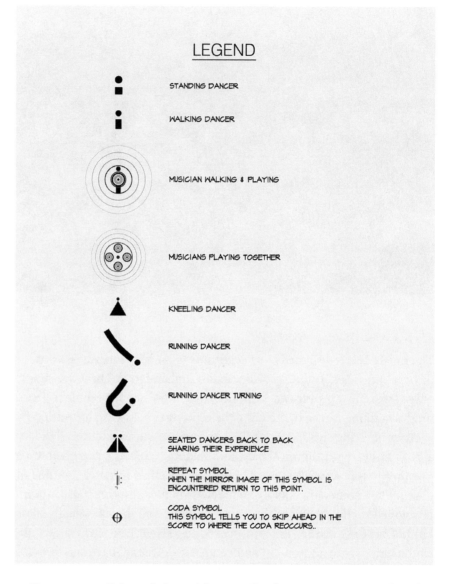

LEGEND

STANDING DANCER

WALKING DANCER

MUSICIAN WALKING & PLAYING

MUSICIANS PLAYING TOGETHER

KNEELING DANCER

RUNNING DANCER

RUNNING DANCER TURNING

SEATED DANCERS BACK TO BACK
SHARING THEIR EXPERIENCE

REPEAT SYMBOL
WHEN THE MIRROR IMAGE OF THIS SYMBOL IS
ENCOUNTERED RETURN TO THIS POINT.

CODA SYMBOL
THIS SYMBOL TELLS YOU TO SKIP AHEAD IN THE
SCORE TO WHERE THE CODA REOCCURS..

Space: Selected site, with room for three concentric circles of runners (formed after the run begins).

People: All participants, including people of all ages and abilities.

Activities:

1. Drummer (or similar musician): start a steady beat, neither fast nor slow, in line with the pace rehearsed beforehand with the four pre-selected initiators of the run.

2. Participants in the large initial circle (who may be asked to kneel before the run begins): stand tall one by one, lift your arms to the sky and, with a sound that rises up from your inhalation and soars

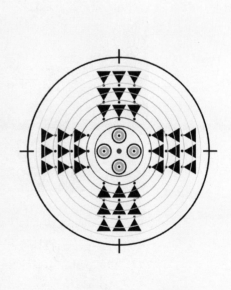

Initial Earth
Run circle, 2015.
Photo © Samara
Daniel-Lindner
Photography.

Billy Cauley blowing
conch shell at start
of Earth Run, 2005.
Photo © John
Kokoska.

out through your exhalation, call out your dedication: "I run for
_____." Then start running counterclockwise to the pulse of
the drum. In this first running circle, the run is vigorous, with long
strides.

3. Once the first circle of runners is established, you may turn left
and reverse direction, forming a smaller circle inside and running
clockwise at a slower, more moderate speed, with shorter strides.
Again, the run (or jog) is always in relation to the drumbeat. At

any time you can switch direction, looping around to move from the slower to the faster circle or vice versa. Take care, though, not to cut off another runner.

4. If you tire, you may turn inward toward the center and form a third circle, moving counterclockwise, at a walking pace in sync with the drumbeat. At any time, if you regain energy, you may loop back to the middle (jogging) circle and then to the fast outer circle. But always keep your steps in relation to the pulse, and never cut across the circles.

5. Once all three circles are established, if you feel you need to rest, you can enter the area inside the third circle, near the musicians, and stand in one of the four directions. You can be still or pulse, but keep your focus on your intention and stay connected to the drumbeat and those around you. Again, at any time, you can reenter the running circles, looping around from walk to jog to fast run. It's important, however, once you have declared your intention and entered the dance, not to go back and stand outside the running circles, as that can break the continuity of the dance.

6. The run continues for as long as the group wishes to run, but long enough for everyone to develop a sense of dedication and determination.

7. When the leader senses the group is finished, a signal is given and the drumbeat fades to a stop. It is time to come to stillness around the musicians. If you are still running, move to the center and join one of the groups already resting in one of the four directions.

8. Once everyone is standing in stillness—following the leader's direction—touch the ground, image the realization of your intention, then rise, place your palms on your heart, and blow your breath into your hands and release it, reaching to the sky, with the sound of "Pah!"—all together as one.

9. For further closure—again, following the leader's direction—sit, close your eyes, and listen to the world around you or to some quiet music or a poem. The leader may also invite you to sit and rest with another person and share your experiences. (This part of the score is relatively open and can be adapted to fit a particular group as needed.)

The Earth Run requires cooperation. It requires group listening to a pulse, and running to that pulse. It requires maintaining a circle, by moving in step with the people in front of you and behind you, being alert and not cutting off other runners. Participants need to understand that this

Taira Restar recalls her experience in 2010, when we celebrated the dance's thirtieth anniversary: "That June morning, surrounded by tall wild flowers and grasses, 400 participants ran in an enormous circle. As I entered the circle of runners, I called out my dedication. I heard others calling out their own dedications. I heard a poet riff on Chief Seattle's speech. 'All things are connected,' he chanted. 'Every step is a prayer.' I concentrated on my own steps one after another after another. Running feet touched the earth. My feet and all the feet ahead of me, behind me, alongside of me touched the earth. Circles of runners—young and old—ran with the pulse of the drum. 'We all breathe the same air.' Inhaling, I breathed in the mountain air. I breathed in the poet's chant. My breath circled into an exhalation. I let go into the concentration of the moment. The circle of runners supported me and I supported them. As my breath paused, I remembered my dedication for the run. Inhaling again, I breathed deeply and felt a surge of renewed energy. Exhaling again, my dedication traveled outward as a prayer. A red-tailed hawk circled above. Utterly focused, I concentrated on my running body—the circling spiral of my body in motion. My right foot and leg moved forward accompanied by my left shoulder, arm, hand. My spine spiraled, rotating in its inner dance. For one blissful moment both feet were off the ground. I was suspended in the clean mountain air. For one moment I was flying. Then I hit the ground running. The ancient dance of sky meets earth was my body. It was all of our bodies. We all were the dance: all 400 runners, 800 feet, the heartbeat of the drums, and the musicians, the poet, the hawk, the sun, the air, and Anna."[17]

is not a competition. Rather, they are being asked to keep a steady pulse; they should move to another lane if they want to run faster or slower.

The structure of the dance itself reminds us of our oneness, and our collective spirit. The dance simply cannot be done without generating a sense of connection in the performers. My hope is that people can set aside their need for "self-expression" and learn to dance for something that is larger than themselves. By simply paying attention to where we are, to all of our senses, to the person in front of you and behind you, to the drumbeat, we have the opportunity to transcend the individual self and join with the larger world.

After one or two Earth Run scores—depending on whether we separate or combine the intentions to run for someone in your life and to run for something in the world—we do a children's run. The children lead off the run, racing around in a large circle. Whenever they feel like it, they

Participants in Earth Run, 2016. Photo © John Vigran, wildheartpictures .com.

Participants in Earth Run, 2005. Photo © John Kokoska.

"Pah," 2016. Photo © Sue Heinemann.

Sacheen Littlefeather and Sky Road Webb give final blessing, 2015. Photo © Sue Heinemann.

can invite adults to join them in the run. Soon whole families are dancing together. This run is a run for the world's future—and the spirit the children bring to it is invariably uplifting.

AFTER THE EARTH RUN

On Mount Tamalpais, when all the runs are finished, we start a procession out of the space, returning to our initial meeting area. The procession out is different from our entrance, when we are taking in the environmental surroundings. We form two lines and then, two by two, led by the musicians, the participants walk down the middle, looking at and acknowledging everyone they pass.

Now it is time for a social feast. People bring food for lunch, gathering in small groups and sharing not only food but also their experiences and their hopes for the future. It is a time of celebration and bonding. And then it's time to clean up, leaving the environment we've enjoyed as we found it.

THE IMPACT OF THE DANCE

The Earth Run has a relatively simple score, yet it has a surprising power for the participants. This power comes from the intense commitment it encourages. I have seen people run for an hour and a half until they're knocked out from the constant drive. Children sometimes dance until they fall to the ground, exhausted and pleased with themselves. Many diverse groups, including women in prison, war veterans, grieving parents, and people with chronic illness, have been able to speak from their own experiences, in community with one another. I'm always amazed at how something so simple can inspire people to go deeply into the human experience.

There are so many stories of the power of this dance. One year a man from Nigeria joined our dance on Mount Tamalpais. I noticed an incredible intensity as he ran—at times tears streamed down his face. Afterward, when I asked him about his run, he said he was running for his twin brother, John, who had been murdered. When he stood and declared his intention, it was the first time he had spoken his brother's name in the ten years since the murder. For him, the dance was an expression of both sorrow and healing, an honoring of his long-lost brother.

Another time, when I did the *Planetary Dance* with one hundred Israelis and Palestinians at a peace conference, I noticed an older man who wept the entire time, unable to run. He was remembering his father, who had been taken prisoner and never returned. A few years later, to my surprise, I saw him again when we did the *Planetary Dance* in downtown

James Hurd Nixon, who has been part of the *Planetary Dance* since its beginning, tells this personal story about the power of the dance: "My son is an alcoholic. His drinking led to a pretty complete estrangement between us, and he moved to a different state. I didn't see him for many years. A few years ago, when it came time for me to choose what my intention would be—what I would run for—I decided that my dedication would be: 'I run for my son who is an alcoholic, that he find a good life, and for all people with alcoholism, that they find good lives.'

"Not long after that, I got an email from my son saying that he was in therapy and would like to talk with me. I later learned that the police had found him passed out on the side of a highway, almost dead. He wound up living in a residential facility working with a therapist, who diagnosed him as using alcohol as a misguided attempt at self-medication to address an underlying brain chemistry dislocation.

"My son told me that he now felt able to control his alcoholism with a combination of medication and herbal therapy. He wanted me to help him come back and live in the Bay Area. We worked out an arrangement and he now lives a few blocks away from me. He is no longer drinking and is working productively.

"How did dancing for my son in the *Planetary Dance* play into this result? I suppose you could say that I used the *Planetary Dance* to pray for something with all of my body, mind, and spirit and my prayer was answered. Simply put, I prayed a special kind of prayer and my prayer was answered."

San Francisco. This time he stood up and joined the run, dedicating his dance to all young children whose fathers had disappeared in war. He told me his run had restored his memory of his lost father.

At the conference in Israel, I was truly inspired by the power of dance to create peace among people. As one participant described it, "For two hours everyone ran, walked, danced and moved in concentric circles to unify our energies for peace and harmony. We were accompanied by many drums and chanting. We transformed the hall into a powerful energetic joyful exhilarating environment of deep and intensive healing .... We all felt connected, enriched and expanded by this deep experience together."[18]

The *Planetary Dance* brings people of different ages, abilities, and walks of life together and gives them a voice. One time, when we did the dance in a San Francisco park, near where many homeless people con-

Children's *Planetary Dance* facilitated by Jeff Rehg, Oakland, California, 1990. Photographer unknown. Anna Halprin Papers; courtesy of Museum of Performance and Design, San Francisco.

gregate, a street person in a wheelchair joined us. Someone wheeled him into the center area, where he pulsed with the drumbeat. Then, unexpectedly, he stood up and did a repetitive movement with his arm, swinging it back and forth and up. People started picking up on his gesture and soon everyone was repeating it in unison as they danced. This seemingly disempowered person had been completely empowered by the group's awareness of his movement and his humanity.

Another time, when we did the dance in Berkeley, I noticed a woman with a prosthetic leg. How would she be able to enter the run? I decided to see if she wanted to lead off the dance—which she did—setting the pace and amazing all of us with her spirit and determination.

Children take the dance just as seriously as adults. Jeff Rehg, a participant in the *Circle the Earth* dances, brought the Earth Run to children in Oakland for many years. He introduced the intention of the dance as an opportunity to run for something larger than themselves. They dedicated their runs to their families, to different environmental issues, to one another. Their cooperation was beautiful to see. One physically challenged child was doing the run, and he kept falling down as he did it. Whenever this happened, another child would run toward him and help him back to his feet. He kept running and falling and being lifted up again. Everyone thought this was so great that they incorporated falling down and getting up into the dance. The way a group of runners begins to blend and join with one another is part of the magic of this dance.

The children were told that other children in the Bay Area and around the world also were doing the *Planetary Dance*, giving them the spirit of global participation. After they had finished running and were lying on their backs, panting, Jeff asked them to look at the sky, to see themselves as part of the natural world. They released the sound of "Pah!" to the sky, and the dance was done.

When Claudia Cuentas did the *Planetary Dance* with Oakland school-children, they were afraid to call out their intentions, so she had them write their intentions on slips of paper, fold the slips, and put them in a container in the center. The intentions revealed the difficulties of their lives—some children ran for family members who were addicted or in jail. Others ran for fathers who had abused their mothers. The children ran and ran and ran until they could run no more, expressing secrets that really held meaning for them.

That the *Planetary Dance* has a universal appeal, speaking to all kinds of people, is evidenced by the way it has spread around the world. Each year brings news of dances being done elsewhere in the United States and in other countries. Katrin Stelter says that when she first experienced this ritual, "I was touched to find this way to pray—not sitting in a church but being physically, emotionally and mentally involved." In 2000 she began leading yearly *Planetary Dances* in Freiburg, Germany. One year, as the group processed up a hill to the site, light rain started, soon changing into a thunderstorm. "We had to turn around for safety reasons," Stelter recalls. "But we still did the ritual, in a different way, in a shelter. All the elements and all the directions were with us—the fire with thunder and lightning, the earth under our feet, the rain, and the wind. We sang a song for preparation and spent a moment in silence to find our intentions. Then we didn't run but stood in three circles and shouted our wishes out loud and then blew them—'Pah!'—into the air. We acknowledged how nature forced us to find another way to do our ritual."

About 300 miles north of Freiburg, members of the Healing Arts group in Neuss, Germany, have been leading another yearly *Planetary Dance* since 1998. They dance their call for peace and healing at a former NATO missile base, now part of the Museum Insel Hombroich.

In 2015, in honor of my ninety-fifth birthday, graduates of the Tamalpa Institute led *Planetary Dances* from Australia and Korea to England, France, Germany, and other European countries to Argentina, Colombia, and the United States. In Texas, Ana Shoemaker brought the *Plane-*

Marie Larsen recalls her own first encounter with the ritual: "We always say that we will have our event 'rain or shine,' and I remember how cold and wet my first *Planetary Dance* was. You had to keep moving because it was foggy, drizzly, and cold. Drenched dancers, runners, and singers didn't want to stop that year; we kept moving to the beat that the drummer Billy Cauley kept, along with Jasper Redrobe's intonations. My sister all but went into a trance with inspiration."

Planetary Dance facilitated by Tomasz Foltyn at fortieth Krakow Theatrical Reminiscences, Poland, 2015. Photo: Piotr Kubic.

tary Dance to women inside a prison. Once the dance started, Shoemaker reports, "the room burst with dedications, no hesitations." Many women honored their children or voiced their hopes of doing better by their families. "Then the women ran, soared with their arms in the air, rhythmically walked, and paused mindfully in the circles; making a sacred space inside the jail. Each mover was an inspiration to another to keep the energy lifted. We closed with some call-and-response singing, a bit of self-love, and finally a send-off of positive love energy. It was a very touching moment."

In the fall of 2015, the *Planetary Dance* was celebrated as part of the Krakow Theatrical Reminiscences Festival in Poland. "The most incred-

Planetary Dance facilitated by Yoann Boyer, Marseille, France, 2015. Photo © Vincent Lucas.

ible thing on that day was the snow—surprising all of us!" recalls Tomasz Foltyn. "The grass was covered with a white layer of the snow, but we kept doing the ritual. People were cold but very focused and motivated to dance the ritual. As one young girl later told me: 'This dance got to my heart deeply, and I'm really hoping there will be no war in this world.'"

Over and over I hear of people using the *Planetary Dance* as a way of coping with the uncertainties and dangers that their communities are facing. At the time of the 2015 UN climate change conference in Paris, Yoann Boyer sent me the following message:

> After terrorist attacks and many people getting killed, there is a lot of tension in France. People are afraid, sad, and angry, and the authorities are forbidding all actions on behalf of the climate as the country is under serious protection from new attacks. In such a dramatic context, I believed it was important to offer the *Planetary Dance* ... and to trust the spirit to allow us to dance for peace. We did it yesterday and it was one of the most uplifting experiences in community I have experienced. We were downtown in the city of Marseille, and more than sixty people showed up, all dressed with green clothes as a symbol of nature, and we did the entire ritual for more than one hour and fifteen minutes.

I was so moved to witness such an incredible energy being released through the ritual—people claiming their intentions, running for peace, dancing, sharing, experiencing being together and uniting as a community. Many people walking by stopped, intrigued, and even joined the ritual. Kids, migrants, tourists— all united in the oneness.

A few months later, after the terrorist bombing in Belgium, Marie Close began offering a series of *Planetary Dances* in Brussels, continuing for four months. As she later emailed me, at first she was in shock and felt paralyzed, but soon she realized that her community needed a way to express themselves and reconnect. In her words:

I knew that the *Planetary Dance* was a very liberating ritual. But was it going to work in my country? When people are scared, are they going to go out to a park? Will the police let us gather? This is a country where we are not used to making rituals.

On the day we chose, all ages were represented: little babies to old people, lots of kids. We warmed up, we had fun, we were embodying our tensions and images before we worked on the intentions. Then people declared: Peace in the world! Living together! One child simply said: "I wish that everything will be ok this week." All of our intentions were essential. By living through this dramatic situation we were all pushed back to our roots, determined to stand for what really mattered to us in life.

The dance ritual was very joyful, playful, abundant. I remember people shouting new intentions in the middle of the ritual. I saw people releasing little by little in their face, shoulders, and whole body; the tone of their voices was changing into something more determined and trustful ....

I hope this medicinal ritual may become more and more part of our world as a healing, a game, a sharing, a gathering, a piece of art, a place to be yourself with others.

Melanie Nowak told me about a *Planetary Dance* she did for the refugees and citizens in her community in Germany. The mayor of her town opened up the city's castle, so they could dance in its large hall, as the outside weather was stormy. Instructions were given in English, German, and Arabic. "When I looked in the eyes of the people at the ending ritual, as they placed their hands on their hearts, they seemed to be very touched," Nowak said. "Afterward a group of Eritrean refugees came spontaneously with their music and showed their folk dances, then a few from Syria came as well wanting to show their dance, and people from Afghanistan brought their music and danced Afghani style." To me, it sounded like a real honoring of peace through dance.

I have found again and again that what connects these dancers in diverse locations is the desire to come together in community and put their bodies on the line for what we hold most dear—peace, community, health, social change. We do the Earth Run as a simple, powerful way to cast our intentions and to commit ourselves to right action in our lives. Musician Dohee Lee reiterates this: "I have been touched and moved so deeply by how every year the individual intentions and dedications relate to what is happening in the world. The whole time I am drumming, singing, chanting, and my heart is beating with the people running, and I am tearing up witnessing their sincerity. We need this ritual so desperately these days to help us take action for a better life, society, and world."

TOWARD A TRULY GLOBAL DANCE

In my late nineties, after a lifetime of dancing, I think a lot about my legacy. The dance I care most about leaving behind is the *Planetary Dance*. What makes this dance special is not just that it's a dance that everybody can participate in. There are a lot of dances now that encourage participation. The *Planetary Dance* is danced for a purpose. It provides an opportunity for people in a community to voice what's important to them—whether it's healing the sick, caring for the land, ending starvation, connecting opposing factions, or guaranteeing clean water. As the many different *Planetary Dances* that have been done around the world show, the score is open enough to evolve to meet different peoples' needs. I see all these *Planetary Dances* as connected, creating ripples from all the participants' dedication throughout the world. I imagine hundreds of *Planetary Dances* with thousands, even millions, of Planetary Dancers dancing for peace among people and peace with the earth.

Recently I read Sebastian Junger's book *Tribe*. Although his focus is on what happens to combat veterans when they return to our contemporary society, I was struck by his emphasis on people's need for connectedness, for a sense of belonging. He describes some of the rituals American Indians have used to help "heal the psychic wounds of war." He goes on to state, "Contemporary America is a secular society that obviously can't just borrow from Indian culture to heal its own psychic wounds. But the spirit of community healing and connection that forms the basis of these ceremonies is one that a modern society might draw on."[19] One reason I believe the *Planetary Dance* has sparked and spread is that it speaks to

Impromptu variation of *Planetary Dance* in "Peace Dove" at a workshop led by Anna at Moa Oasis, Israel, 2014. Photo © Sue Heinemann.

this need for healing and connection. In some sense, I see it as a dance of survival. Our civilization is in a dire situation, with ongoing wars, divisiveness, and the destruction of our planet as a place that can sustain humanity and the other species whose lives are intertwined with our own. The *Planetary Dance* provides a means of expressing our concern about these threats as a group and gathering the strength to take action.

The *Planetary Dance* is a global dance that transcends cultural and temporal barriers, a dance that speaks to the needs of the community that makes it, and a dance that addresses contemporary issues, such as peace, conflict, illness, and the needs of our future generations, as they are experienced by all people on this planet. It is a dance for the benefit of others, a calling in which we ask for the power to bring about a positive result. Through the *Planetary Dance* we can bring our everyday lives—our relationships, concerns, and work—into the context of something extraordinary.[20]

Conclusion

Run with It!

Twenty-some years ago when this book was first started, I had no idea how the search for living myths and rituals would unfold. The first draft of the book was entirely about *Circle the Earth: Dancing with Life on the Line*, because in its time it was the most evolved exploration of living myths that I had done. I had no idea that the answer to the search I had been on my whole life—for a dance as meaningful to me as my grandfather's dance was to him—was right in front of me. And of course I was unaware of how, in the several decades since we did *Circle the Earth*, the world would continue to spiral out of control with violence, ecological degradation, war, global warming, and other perils for life on earth. I had no idea that a small part of *Circle the Earth*—the Earth Run—would develop into such a meaningful global ritual.

As far as myths and rituals go, both the *Planetary Dance* and *Circle the Earth* are very young. Most rituals take centuries to come into the fullness of their being, fed by experience and nurtured by their continuous re-creation in the communities they serve. Through this process, a living myth and ritual provides structure and scaffold for a community, as well as an opportunity for unity and group expression. I see *Circle the Earth* and the *Planetary Dance* in a lineage with the very beginnings of dance, when dance was a means of maintaining community, fostering healing, and connecting with the environment. Only time will tell if *Circle the Earth* and the *Planetary Dance* will continue to serve this need.

The persistence of these particular dances is not the most important thing. What is key is the *process* of making dances that matter, bringing communities together to explore real-life issues and to take concerted, collective action in response. How you carry on with these dances and the scoring process and adapt the basic structures to your own community is what counts. There is a pressing need for all of us to take action against the numerous threats we face. For me, community dance ritual offers one way to do this. It engages actively with the social context and the mystery of our intentions. It is no accident that the *Planetary Dance* has evolved into a dance for peace with the planet. The numerous ways we can interpret that broad statement—"peace with the planet"—turns out to include ecological justice; the cessation of war and violence; the union of people from different cultures, ideologies, and religious identities; and so many other deep social issues. It is critical that citizen artists create contemporary dance rituals that involve communities of people in their making. It is time for dance, for art, and for the power of people in community to be used in ways that serve our day-to-day lives, that help us make sense of the overwhelming challenges of this time, to live into the future with what the great Buddhist scholar Joanna Macy calls "active hope." It has been my experience that these rituals support this quest for community groups that are taking a stand for life on earth.

What I see as pivotal in a dance like *Circle the Earth* is that performers live through their real-life experiences as the dance unfolds, so that their physical and emotional responses are based in their reality. While this is not a dance "technique" in the traditional sense of the word, it is a discipline that requires a balance of movement, emotions, and images, while remaining open and available to the moment of their unfolding. Staying awake to these many layers of our being—our physical, mental, spiritual, and emotional bodies, as well as the body of the collective—is a "technique" in itself, and this is what we teach when we perform dances like *Circle the Earth* or the *Planetary Dance*. All the skill-building scores in this book are part of this process of cultivating attention, creating relationships, and deepening our contact with ourselves and the world around us.

I have often wondered why the *Planetary Dance* has become so popular, spreading around the globe from its original home on Mount Tamalpais. What is it that makes it so compelling to so many people all around the world? The dance seems to strike a chord in people, regardless of our cultural differences, feeding our common desires to be unified, to celebrate our diversity, and to take communal actions that create change. It is clear that as a human community we need to come into a balanced relationship to one another and the earth in order to survive. One hope lies in the creation of symbolic systems, stories, and rituals that support our need for connection, contact, and continuity. We need to write new stories, make new dances, and instigate ritual actions that speak to our lives, now. We can become despairing over the loss of traditional forms

Jahan Khalighi and Dohee Lee lead a *Planetary Dance* at the opening of the fifty-seventh International Art Exhibition of La Biennale di Venezia, Italy, 2017. Photo © Alessandro Illuzzi.

and the fragmentation of modern life, or we can grasp the nature of the situation and take positive action. Our differences are many, but so are our commonalities. Coming into alignment with each other by acknowledging both individual and collective needs, the way we do in dances like *Circle the Earth* and the *Planetary Dance*, offers us an opportunity as modern people to join with others in causes we share.

I believe a deeper understanding of the practices of dance and ritual serves our lives in fundamental ways toward these ends. The kind of dance I am advocating utilizes forms and structures rooted in all of human history and culture. They are akin to my grandfather's dance, or the indigenous dances of the native people of this continent, in their capacity to unify people in common cause. This kind of dance can connect us to part of what we are in danger of losing—the diversity of the earth, the power of the body, and the human drive to connect. We live in a time where the old world is dropping away to make room for the new, yet we need some of the wisdom of the past in order to survive. I make these dances because I believe that our current options and experiences are related to older cultural practices and a specific devotion to the stories of the body. Dances like *Circle the Earth* create new options and new ways of looking at our lives. These dances provide the literal experience of breaking out of the habitual patterns of fear and isolation that constrain our lives, our relationships to one another, and the earth. It is possible to create something else: awareness, safety, intimacy, healing, and community. And the first step in imagining another possibility is actually experiencing it.

One of the key lessons I have learned in the process of creating dance rituals is that people of all backgrounds can participate and that this participation enhances all of our lives. I deeply believe in a Life/Art Process that reveals itself through the mythology of the self and expands in its application to the mythology of the collective body. I believe this creates a bigger circle in which we can all dance, a circle that simultaneously acknowledges our differences and the forces that bind our lives together. Ritual-making is a process with an inherent value system and a means of making actual that which is now only potential. In both *Circle the Earth* and the *Planetary Dance*, we create a collective body and a unified spirit by infusing our individual personal experiences into our dance. *Circle the Earth* and the *Planetary Dance* can be catalysts for the re-creation of new myths and rituals, a model for other purposeful dances for diverse communities. By dancing our life issues, we bring about change because the dance truly does change the dancer.

In the past few decades I have met more and more young dancers and theater-makers who are creating work that is responsive to their communities' needs and experiences. Our strained social and economic circumstances are pushing artists to ask: What matters? What do my people need? What do we want? How can we live better on this earth? And to make work from that place. This gives rise to a more pertinent and necessary art with an impetus to create change—in the performer, the audience, and the world—as well as to express political and social concerns. Dancers are beginning to grasp the concept that dance can be not only beautiful, but also educative, initiatory, transformative, and healing.

If you are one of these dancers, I encourage you to keep in mind that the more resources you have as community leaders, the more powerful your dances will become. Do not squander the resources that reside within your community—the people who have gathered skills of organizing, facilitating, communicating, and loving the world where they live. Bring the best you've got to what you care most about and keep asking yourself the open question: What are the resources I bring to bear on this situation? How can I bring my community together to create an impact?

Find your best route toward taking a stance on behalf of yourself and your community.

Circle the Earth and the *Planetary Dance* are part of a long search for the maps we need to take us to the places we want to go. They are part of a growing vision for myths and rituals that can serve us now. I imagine many new dances for us to do—dances of sexual liberation to remind us of the beauty and life force of the body; dances between mothers and daughters, between fathers and sons; dances with animals and trees to remind us that we're not the center of the universe but part of its circle; dances to celebrate birth and to mourn death; dances to heal the sick and to celebrate union; dances to identify and clarify our grief and our love. I see us dancing the hard dances until they become easy, stumbling and tripping over each other until we learn to dance together again. For all my life, I have been looking for a dance with as much meaning as the one that motivated my grandfather and his community so long ago. It gives me deep pleasure to recognize that while we cannot return to the traditional innocence of my grandfather's dance, we can create dances in its spirit, dances that confront the issues that matter deeply to us.

I see this all as a wonderful possibility and a great hope. I offer up the fruit of my many decades of exploration in dance, community, and the environment to support your community challenges. I send this book out into the world hoping that the same processes of generating collective creativity that inspired *Circle the Earth* and the *Planetary Dance* will encourage the creation of all the dances we need to learn to live gracefully with one another and the planet that is our home.

APPENDIX A. Leading a *Planetary Dance*

This appendix offers some additional guidelines for leading a *Planetary Dance* in your community.[21] For a successful event, we strongly recommend you contact the Tamalpa Institute (www.tamalpa.org), which offers the only certified training for *Planetary Dance* leaders and which can try to connect you with an experienced leader in your area.

I. HOW TO START THE EVENT

1. **Arrival.** Know who might be coming and the space in which you will be working. Do what you can to prepare participants to exit everyday life and enter a special consciousness, a shared experience. This might include greeters, signs, flags, specially chosen music, silence, food sharing, or a printed program. Your attitude is most important in setting the tone.

2. **Welcome Everyone.** This is your introduction and can include introducing others, such as guest leaders, facilitators, musicians, poets, or educators.

3. **Tell the Story.** Tell the story of the *Planetary Dance*, its history and its legacy of peace. Determine the length and storytelling style appropriate for your audience. You can tell the story of the evolution of the dance itself, or you can tell the story of how you came to decide to offer the *Planetary Dance* in your own community.

4. **Share Your Theme for the Event.** State the power this theme holds for you and why you chose it. You can connect this theme—the *collective intention*—to the story. Ask participants about their *personal intention* in doing the Earth Run. What is important in their lives? This can be shared out loud, between participant pairs, in writing, or in silent thought. The crafting of individual intentions deserves some time; don't rush this part. The more connected people are to their intentions, the more powerful the dance will be. Remember this is a dance ritual dedicated to benefit others and the planet. It is not intended solely for personal healing.

II. HOW TO TRAIN PARTICIPANTS BEFORE THE RUN

1. **Introduce and Describe the Earth Run Score.** It is helpful to show a graphic score and then have a few people actually demonstrate how you make a group circle and move in and out of different circles without disturbing the flow (see steps 4 and 5 below). Make sure to frame the Earth Run as a living dance, always evolving, shaped by the people who perform it.

2. **Train the Breath and the Pulse.** You will need a drummer (or similar pulse-setting musician). Set the beat with clapping and/or stepping. Have trained facilitators demonstrate. It is the power of moving collectively to the pulse that sends our intentions out into the world. Train your participants to move with a common pulse. It is the collective energy of everyone moving to the same beat that generates a transcendent energy.

3. **Discuss the Intention and Pulse.** You have already introduced the theme. Now describe how, using the common beat or pulse, participants will be carrying this theme as a powerful collective intention. Creating this incredible power comes from the focus of intention. Give examples of how participants can state intentions clearly. Also demonstrate how they can forcefully voice their intentions as they exhale. If you are planning to do three runs, the first intention might call for the healing of someone or some situation you know directly and the second for healing on a more global scale. The third run could be a children's run, or a run for another special group.

4. **The Circle.** Explain that joining hands together in a circle is a reflection of unity. The circle has no beginning and no end, no leader and no follower. It can represent the cycles of life. You can describe the circles of the score, demonstrate with trained runners, and/or show posters graphically depicting the score.

5. **The Run.** Describe or demonstrate how to change speed and directions. As runners tire, they can move to a slower, smaller circle moving in the opposite direction. They can return to a faster circle at any time. Or they might rest in the area around the musicians and then rejoin the run. Show how to keep space between runners and how to keep space between circles.

6. **The Pause in the Four Directions.** If you mark the four directions (which is optional), you can describe how runners might pause in one of the four directions. You might explain that the journey of the sun marks east and west. The journey of the seasons marks north and south. Elaborate as meaningful to you and your group. Participants can choose a direction that holds power for them in which to pause—a place to rest and absorb the power of the dance and of the direction. The four directions create a square within the circle to form a mandala, sacred to many cultures, a geometric representation of the universe.

7. **The Final Stop.** Indicate that you will signal the dancers and drumbeat to come to a final stop once the power has built and an energetic climax has been reached. Everyone should naturally gather together to rest, coming into the center circle.

8. **Touch the Earth.** Tell participants that you will then ask them to slowly reach or kneel down to touch the earth and image their dedication becoming a reality.

9. **The Pah!** Explain that at the very end you will invite everyone to rise up to a standing position, throw their arms overhead, and vocalize a "Pah!" sound, signaling a personal and collective message being sent out to the world.

10. **Exit to Enter.** Give the participants time to attend to personal needs (bathroom, water, clothing, and the like)—their exit—and prepare them to enter the dance circle. Silence and procession are options.

III. HOW TO PREPARE THE SPACE

Make sure that the running space is free of obstacles and offers a relatively even surface, without holes or other impediments. Figure out where the circles and the four directions will be before the group arrives.

1. **The Center Circle.** This is where the leader and the drummers (and other musicians) will be.

2. **The Four Directions.** Ideally, these should be marked at the edge of the large circle. They can be defined with flags, banners, or something similar.

3. **The Large Circle.** This is where the participants will begin their run.

4. **The Running Space.** These inner dance circles are the smaller concentric circles where dancers will run and walk to the pulse as the dance proceeds.

IV. HOW TO LEAD THE DANCE

1. **Enter the Center Circle as Leader and Drummer(s).** Options include ritualizing this with a procession and music, entering as the large circle forms, or entering afterward.

2. **Create the Large Circle.** Optionally, you may request participants to enter in procession, in silence, to music, through an archway, or something similar. You may choose to define this area by asking the participants to hold hands as they proceed to form the circle or in some other way. Once formed and aligned with the center circle, the area can be marked with flour, colored sand, or another material. (If you are dancing in a particularly windy area, choose a material that will not blow away.) Note that nothing on the dance surface should interfere with the safety of the participants or damage the surface.

3. **Clarify the Four Directions.** Use trained flag bearers or other facilitators to stand in the four directions, defining them for participants. *Note*: You may choose to change the order of steps 1, 2, and 3 or to make them simultaneous.

4. **Announce the Opening.** One of the musicians blows a horn or a conch shell in each of the four directions to open the Earth Run. Participants may remain standing, or the leader may signal everyone to kneel or sit.

5. **Begin the Pulse.** The leader signals the start of the drumbeat. (You should rehearse the pulse with the main drummer and initial runners before starting.) The main drummer needs to be able to hold the pulse even when

other musicians join in. And all the musicians must remain synchronized to the pulse beat.

6. **Begin the Run with Intentions.** It is best to select several people to start off the run, modeling the dedication, the counterclockwise direction of the initial running circle, and the spacing between runners. Practice with these runners ahead of time, at the site, and with the drummer. Because running surfaces can vary, they need to know what they will be running on beforehand—as that may change their run. After the initial running circle is established, participants can turn to run at a slower pace in a smaller circle in the opposite (clockwise) direction. They can later turn to enter a third circle of walkers, moving counterclockwise inside the other two circles.

7. **Allow a Pause.** As runners tire, they may rest in the area around the musicians, or in one of the four directions (if these are marked), and absorb the power of their experience.

8. **Indicate the Final Stop.** Signal participants to rest and then invite them to join the group in the center circle. Practice beforehand with your drummer how to signal this.

9. **Touch the Earth.** Invite dancers to kneel or reach down to touch the earth and to visualize their intentions coming true.

10. **Rise to the Sky with a Pah!** Signal dancers to rise and collectively send their dedications out to the world.

V. OPTIONS FOR BRINGING THE GROUP TO CLOSURE

1. **Sharing with a Partner.** Use your voice and timing to help participants absorb their experience and integrate it into their lives. You might invite every participant to find a partner, sit back-to-back on the ground, and describe to each other what they ran for and what the experience meant to them.

2. **Offerings.** You may want to facilitate integration with gentle music or chanting. A professional whistler, a poet, or a violinist might add an inspirational ending. You might also include drawings and dialogue.

3. **Closure.** Depending on your space, you may want to create a procession out to a socializing area. This is also a time for focusing the energy created by the dance through networking, distributing printed information, requesting donations for causes, and the like.

4. **Food Sharing.** Food plays a vital role in all cultures. Sharing food and water replenishes the body and soul. It bonds a culture. As an option, this step may precede or accompany steps 2 or 3.

VI. SPECIAL CONSIDERATIONS FOR
A *PLANETARY DANCE* WITH CHILDREN

If you are interested in leading a *Planetary Dance* for a group of children, here are some ideas for modifying the score.[22]

1. **Add Visual Art.** A visual art exercise helps children process the experience and integrate its meaning into their own lives.

2. **Offer Extra Preparation.** If possible, meet with the children once or twice before the dance or make the dance part of a special workshop. You might share a short version of the story of the dance, teach them the breath and the pulse, and give them time to draw, paint, or write about their personal intention. In a special workshop you might design fun scores that encourage them to connect with the natural environment, perhaps by dancing as a favorite animal.

3. **Adapt for Skill Levels.** Children under ten may find it hard to remember to run on the beat, so you might encourage them to run freely and in only one direction.

4. **Consider Inviting the Parents to Participate.** Engaging parents and children together can enhance the experience for both. Take care to make the activities appealing to fathers and sons as well as daughters and mothers.

5. **Include a Food Ritual.** Children love to create a special ceremony around a meal, helping to prepare it and present it in a unique way.

APPENDIX B. Questions to Ask in Planning a *Planetary Dance*

An effective *Planetary Dance* requires a lot of advance planning. Here are some questions to help you along the way.[23]

1. **Why?** Why do you want to organize a *Planetary Dance*? In other words: What intention is motivating you, and what do you hope to accomplish?

2. **Who?** Who is the community that you intend to work with? Is the dance for the general public? For students at a school? For the participants of a conference, seminar, or workshop?
    What are the characteristics of the participants (e.g., age, background, common purpose)?
    How many people do you envision participating?
    Who will be part of your planning team, helping to choose the special theme of the dance and liaising with the community? Who will help publicize the event? Do you need a fundraiser?
    And who will be part of your facilitating team at the event? Who will first greet people coming for the event? Who can best warm up the participants and introduce the score? Who should start and model the run? Who are your musicians? Are there special guest artists who can inspire with offerings?

3. **Where?** What kind of space best suits the community you envision participating? Should the dance be held indoors or outdoors? And if outdoors, is there an environment that can help contain the event, providing clear boundaries?
    Do you want to prepare people in one space and then process to another for the Earth Run?
    Does the space you have chosen have any special requirements, such as permits, grass cutting or raking, or insurance?

4. **When?** Which date and time are most convenient for the people you want to invite and the venue you have chosen?
    How long do you anticipate the event lasting? What is your schedule for the event? How much time should each aspect take, from introductions and preparation for the run, to the run itself, and then closure and sharing afterward?

5. **What?** What is your special theme for the event and how is it related to your community?
    What scores will best prepare your participants for the Earth Run?
    What kinds of special offerings might provide inspiration?

6. **How?** Have you worked out a production timeline? Starting with your event date and working backward, what is your target date for the tasks that need to be completed to keep your event on track? When, for example, do you need to send out various forms of publicity?

   How will you publicize your event? Do you, for example, need postcards, flyers, or posters? Do you have a press release and a list of press contacts? Will an email blast be effective? Do you have a strategy for sharing on social media?

   What special equipment (if any) do you need for the event? Do you, for example, need to rent a PA system or extra toilet facilities? Should you bring water for participants? What about a first-aid kit?

   What is your budget for the event and how will you raise any necessary funds?

NOTES

1. Many of my dances have also evolved out of the Life/Art Process, including *City Dance, Blank Placard Dance*, and *Ceremony of Us*, which are detailed in my book *Moving toward Life: Five Decades of Transformational Dance* (Middletown, CT: Wesleyan University Press, 1995).
2. For a more in-depth discussion of the Life/Art Process, see Daria Halprin, *The Expressive Body in Life, Art and Therapy: Working with Movement, Metaphor and Meaning* (London: Jessica Kingsley, 2003).
3. For further information on the creation of *Ceremony of Us*, see my book *Moving toward Life*, 152–68, and the film *Right On/Ceremony of Us* (see www.anna halprin.org).
4. Daria Halprin, *The Expressive Body*, 17–18.
5. For a detailed explanation of the RSVP Cycles, see Lawrence Halprin, *The RSVP Cycles: Creative Processes in the Human Environment* (New York: George Braziller, 1969).
6. For more detail on these explorations, see my book *Moving toward Life*.
7. The Tamalpa Institute, which I cofounded with my eldest daughter, Daria Halprin, offers training in movement-based expressive arts education and therapy (www.tamalpa.org). It is the only certified training organization for people interested in learning how to create community dance rituals using the RSVP Cycles and the Life/Art Process.
8. For a more detailed discussion of the *Planetary Dance*, see chapter 4 in this book. A history of the *Planetary Dance* also appears in my book *Moving toward Life*.
9. We suggest that anyone who is planning to take on a community dance ritual of this scope get some training beyond reading this book. The Tamalpa Institute offers the only certified training in the Halprin Life/Art Process.
10. Time, space, people, and activities are the four elements of a score. The time dimension is often the most fluid, depending on how many people are in the group and the intention you have for the score itself. Feel free to change this variable to suit your needs.
11. Lauren Artress, *Walking a Sacred Path: Discovering the Labyrinth as a Spiritual Practice* (New York: Riverhead Books, 1995, rev. 2006).
12. Although at the time I called this the Snake Dance, with its sinuous line from the "head" to the "tail," I no longer use this name. When I showed this dance to my Pomo Indian friends, they were upset by the snake reference, which held strong cultural associations for them. It taught me a lot about the need to be attentive to cultural differences.
13. This poem was first introduced by the poet Kush, with variations by Allan Stinson and music by Grant Rudolph.

14. In 1851 Seattle, chief of the Suquamish and other Indian tribes around Washington's Puget Sound, delivered what is considered to be one of the most beautiful and profound environmental statements ever made. "How can you buy or sell the sky, the warmth of the land?" he reportedly asked, adding: "Every part of the earth is sacred to my people."

15. Daniel K. Stat, "Double-Chambered Whistling Bottles: A Unique Peruvian Pottery Form," *Journal of Transpersonal Psychology* 2 (1974): 157–62; http://www.peruvianwhistles.com/journ-transpersonal.html.

16. Poem © 2017 Jahan Khalighi.

17. Taira Restar, "Dancing the Planet," *Animated: The Community Dance Magazine* (Autumn 2010): 16.

18. "Women Walk for Middle East Peace," November 5, 2010; https://uri.org/uri-story/20101105-women-walk-middle-east-peace.

19. Sebastian Junger, *Tribe: On Homecoming and Belonging* (New York and Boston: Twelve, 2016), 121.

20. Adapted from Anna Halprin, "Planetary Dance," in *Moving toward Life*, 236.

21. These guidelines are adapted from ones given by Anna Halprin, Suki Munsell, and Jamie McHugh in *The Planetary Dance Handbook*, used by the Tamalpa Institute in its training program.

22. Adapted from section by Marguerite Etemad in *The Planetary Dance Handbook*.

23. Adapted from sections by Jamie McHugh and Marie Larsen in *The Planetary Dance Handbook*.

ADDITIONAL RESOURCES

On the Halprin approach to creativity, dance, and healing, see the websites www
.annahalprin.org and www.tamalpa.org, as well as the following books and films.
For more on the *Planetary Dance*, see the website www.planetarydance.org.

BOOKS

Halprin, Anna. *Movement Ritual*, illus. Charlene Koonce. Kentfield, CA: San
    Francisco Dancers' Workshop/Tamalpa Institute, 1979.
———. *Moving toward Life: Five Decades of Transformational Dance*, ed. Rachel
    Kaplan. Middletown, CT: Wesleyan University Press, 1995.
———. *Returning to Health with Dance, Movement and Imagery*. Mendocino,
    CA: LifeRhythm, 2002.
Halprin, Daria. *The Expressive Body in Life, Art and Therapy: Working with
    Movement, Metaphor and Meaning*. London: Jessica Kingsley, 2003.
Halprin, Lawrence. *The RSVP Cycles: Creative Process in the Human Environment*.
    New York: George Braziller, 1969.
Halprin, Lawrence, and Jim Burns. *Taking Part: A Workshop Approach to
    Collective Creativity*. Cambridge, MA: MIT Press, 1974.
Ross, Janice. *Anna Halprin: Experience as Dance*. Berkeley: University of
    California Press, 2007.
Wittmann, Gabriele, Ursula Schorn, and Ronit Land. *Anna Halprin: Dance—
    Process—Form*. London: Jessica Kingsley, 2014.
Worth, Libby, and Helen Poynor. *Anna Halprin*. London: Routledge, 2004.

FILMS
See www.annahalprin.org for links to trailers.

Breath Made Visible: Revolution in Dance / Anna Halprin, by Ruedi Gerber,
    ZAS Films, 2009, 80 minutes.
Circle the Earth: Dancing with Life on the Line, directed by Anna Halprin,
    produced by Media Arts West, 1989, 40 minutes.
Dance for Your Life: STEPS Theatre Company for People Challenging AIDS, directed
    by Anna Halprin, produced by David Karp, 1988, 32 minutes.
Positive Motion: Challenging AIDS Through Dance, by Andy Abrahams Wilson,
    Open Eye Pictures, 1991, 37 minutes.
*Returning Home: Moving with the Earth Body / Learning Lessons in Life, Loss
    and Liberation*, by Andy Abrahams Wilson, Open Eye Pictures, 2003, 45
    minutes.

ACKNOWLEDGMENTS

This book could never have happened without the support of the many friends and colleagues who have contributed their time and advice over many years, and to all of them I am deeply grateful. I especially want to thank my cowriter Rachel Kaplan, whose decisive insight and understanding of dance lend clarity and heart to this book. Rachel brings her knowledge as an experienced dancer, a somatic and expressive arts therapist, the author of the reader-friendly guide *Urban Homesteading*, and the editor of my previous books, *Moving toward Life* and *Dance as a Healing Art*. Not only did she encourage me to complete this book (in the works for twenty-some years), but she did all she could to make sure it happened.

Also instrumental in the creation of this book was Allan Stinson. A longtime collaborator and dear friend, he helped develop *Circle the Earth: Dancing with Life on the Line*. His poetic genius, wide heart, and dedication to that large and complex project were critical in bringing it to fruition. Much of chapter 3 in this book derives from Allan's writings about *Circle the Earth*, as well as taped discussions he had with me about this project. Allan died of AIDS. I will always honor his brilliance, talent, and enduring spirit.

Also deserving special thanks are editor Sue Heinemann, for her perceptive suggestions and tireless assistance in shaping and fine-tuning the manuscript as well as gathering photographs, and graphic designer Brian Collentine, for his keen eye and striking cover design. My daughters Daria Halprin and Rana Halprin gave generously of their time in reviewing the manuscript and providing valuable feedback, as did my longtime collaborators James Nixon and Jamie McHugh. I am also grateful to all the photographers who have allowed us to use their images; to my assistant Stephanie Earle and to Kirsten Tanaka of San Francisco's Museum of Performance and Design for their help in collecting important archival material; to my assistant Sherri Mills for documenting the Planetary Dance Certification Workshop; and to Suzanna Tamminen of Wesleyan University Press for advocating for this book and guiding it through the publishing process.

Over the years the hundreds of people who have taken part in *Circle the Earth* and the *Planetary Dance* have both inspired me and contributed to the evolution of these dances. The participation of the brave members of Positive Motion (men challenging AIDS), Women with Wings (women challenging AIDS), and the Moving Towards Life group made *Circle the Earth: Dancing with Life on the Line* possible. I remember with affection and appreciation all the dancers who shared their stories, their courage, and their camaraderie through the process of creating these dances.

In the introduction I described how, as a child, I witnessed my grandfather's passionate dance in the house of prayer. For me, the *Planetary Dance* has become the one dance that means as much to me as his dance meant to him —

and so I am deeply indebted to all the people who have assisted me with this dance, both locally and around the world. I am continually delighted to learn of students and colleagues who have performed the *Planetary Dance* in their own communities and to hear their stories about the experience. Without the many years of monthly meetings of the Planetary Dance Committee, our yearly event on Mount Tamalpais in Marin County could never have evolved so lovingly and spread to so many places. I want to thank James Nixon, the committee chair and closely involved since the start, along with longtime committee members Russell Bass, Marguerite Etemad, Sue Heinemann, Marie Larsen, Lynn Moody, Suki Munsell, and Stephen Grossberg, whose graphic score has been widely replicated and was central to the *Planetary Dance* installation at the 57th International Art Exhibition of La Biennale di Venezia. The *Planetary Dance* in Marin owes much to the steady dedication of its musicians, especially master drummer Barbara Borden, who hasn't missed a beat since its birth, along with many others, including Billy Cauley, Dohee Lee, Benito Santiago, and my grandson Jahan Khalighi, who has attended the *Planetary Dance* since he was a child. I am also thankful for the many blessings given at this dance by Sacheen Littlefeather and Jasper Redrobe, who also gave me the big drum we use and the eagle feather for smudging the children. For me, the participation of children brings a special joy, as they are our future. So it has been immensely meaningful for me that over the years, in addition to Jahan, my grandchildren Micah and LeVanna Vassau have joined many Planetary Dances. In recent years my granddaughter Ruthanna Brill has brought the next generation—my great-grandchildren Ella Rose and Nathan—to run with us.

It personally gives me great satisfaction that the Tamalpa Institute under the direction of Daria Halprin has sponsored the *Planetary Dance* throughout the years and has begun to offer certified training for *Planetary Dance* leaders. I am confident that the Tamalpa Institute will help this peace dance thrive and facilitate its spread around the world.

Recognizing that certain ideas planted in early years mature and evolve as time moves on, I also want to acknowledge the impact of my dance studies with Margaret H'Doubler at the University of Wisconsin. Her inspiring teaching led me to a vision of dance as an art accessible to all people. I am forever grateful for the foundation she set many years ago.

And finally, I could not have done any of this work without the support and collaboration of my husband, Lawrence Halprin. *Circle the Earth* and the *Planetary Dance* had their origins in a community workshop we led together. Most important, the RSVP Cycle process he developed sets out principles of creativity that have guided me through all my work. I cannot thank him enough.

INDEX

Page numbers in *italics* refer to illustrations.

ABOUT THE AUTHORS

Anna Halprin's diverse career has spanned the field of dance since the late 1930s, creating revolutionary directions for the art form and inspiring fellow choreographers to take modern dance to new dimensions. A dance innovator, she was an early pioneer in the use of movement/dance as a healing art. She founded the groundbreaking San Francisco Dancers' Workshop in 1955 and the Tamalpa Institute in 1978 with her daughter Daria Halprin. She is the author of several books, including *Moving toward Life*, published by Wesleyan University Press in 1995.

Rachel Kaplan is a psychotherapist, political activist, and permaculture designer. She is the author of *Urban Homesteading: Heirloom Skills for Sustainable Living* and *The Probable Site of the Garden of Eden*. She edited Anna Halprin's *Moving toward Life* and has worked closely with her on all her book projects since the mid-1990s.